Investment in Innovation

prepared for the Science and Industry Committee by

C. F. Carter and B. R. Williams

Vice-Chancellor, University of Lancaster
Vice-Chancellor and Principal, University of Sydney

Macdonald . London

© Oxford University Press 1958
© C. F. Carter & B. R. Williams 1971

First published in 1958 by
Oxford University Press

This unabridged edition first published in 1971 by
Macdonald & Co. (Publishers) Ltd
49–50 Poland Street
London, W.1

SBN 356 03487 9

PRINTED AND BOUND IN ENGLAND BY
HAZELL WATSON AND VINEY LTD
AYLESBURY, BUCKS

The New Manager's Library
General Editor: D. R. C. Halford, o.b.e.

Investment in Innovation

The New Manager's Library

Apologia

During some twenty years in Industry, I have had to read a large number of management books of one sort and another—many connected with my work, but many outside it.

Among all of these there have been only a handful which have kept my interest and made a lasting impression; other people's experience must be much the same. So, when asked to take over the editorship of this series, I was glad of the opportunity to try to do what I could to add to the number; and to introduce some of my favourites to a wider audience.

I have often felt that the man who most needs to learn is exactly the man for whom very little is written. The new manager is usually among the keenest to know and understand what goes on—but he is very poorly treated by the usual run of academic dispute, of advice from adepts to experienced practitioners, and of superficial introductions to various subjects. The new manager wants very little of these; if they are all that is offered, he is likely to cry 'to the devil with both your houses', and to carry on his work by whatever light his nature casts. A loss, not only to him, but to business as a whole.

The books in this series are all specifically addressed to the new manager and his problems. The most immediate of these problems are those of getting on with colleagues in other functions—in all but the smallest of companies the invisible walls which surround functional empires tend to be tall and impenetrable; and arguments on who does what on the imperial frontiers are not of concern only to the Trade Unions. So, one task of the Library will be to describe other people's jobs—what goes on behind some of the closed doors along the corridor. There are problems there, too, and the apparently contentious conflicts which come through the door are usually due to the logic of the problems and not to backstairs intrigue by those on the other side, nor even to ordinary cussedness.

Quite apart from this effort to bring understanding and so promote co-operation on the business scene, there are at least two other reasons why an awareness of other people's jobs will be useful. First, a broader outlook should counter parochialism, and plant a few doubts on whether super-efficiency at one's own job regardless of anything else is ever the right thing in the general interest.

More importantly, an understanding of the problems of all the functions is a very good key to the door leading to general management—if not the only one. It is, really, only generalists like accountants who have to have this essential equipment of a general manager as part of their work; it might be a good thing for the specialists to indulge in some extra-curricular activity, to acquire the qualifications too—and it will probably be in this country's best interests also, because there is a lot of talent outside accountancy, which tends to wither in a subordinate role.

The other set of problems is how best to deal with the job in hand. To the beginner, there appears to be an immense tool-bag, filled to overflowing with a vast range of techniques, each with its own vociferous crowd proclaiming its merits—and with an equally large crowd busily denigrating it. But it is surprising how far one can get with no more than a hammer, a screwdriver, a pair of pliers, a vice, a saw, some chisels, a drill, a plane, and a few assorted files.

There are only a few vital techniques which, when used with common sense, are all that is needed to solve most problems. So, the other task of the Library will be to describe these fundamental techniques, to show what they can do, what they cannot do, what dangers attend their use, and what has to be done if something more complex is needed.

Finally, since all business is a story about people, the books will not allow themselves to forget them, with all their complexities—which does not mean an unpalatable dose of the social sciences. What it does mean is that any conclusion amply proved in practice will be incorporated into the Library's outlook, whether it comes from the physical or the social sciences, or from some more commonplace source. This is very far from meaning that only the established truth will be revealed; much of the Library will be concerned with fresh insights, and will let the controversy fall where it will.

No one, not even the authors of books in the Library (and certainly not its general editor), knows more than a small fraction of the truth. Anyone, particularly those at the start of their careers in management, can have good and workable new ideas, given the stimulus.

Investment in Innovation is (still) a heretic's book. Anyone will find strong support for any rebellion they have in mind on the subject of investment appraisal—support which rests on research into how companies in fact behave.

It is a must for those who really want to start to understand a little about capital expenditure, as well as about innovation; particularly is this so for those who have the gravest doubts on the usefulness of any popular appraisal formulae; and the whole book (the appendix in particular) is almost guaranteed to afford comfort to those who from time to time find themselves the only ones in step.

D. R. C. Halford
General Editor

Contents

Introduction

The term 'investment' which appears in the title of this book refers to the spending of money on the plant, machines and buildings of industry, and on vehicles and other transport facilities. This form of spending is vitally important to economic progress; it is indeed the origin of most increases in wealth, the prime mover which drives industry forward. It is also a type of spending capable of great variation, and its fluctuations can involve the whole economy in the fever of inflation or in depression and decay. So important a part of the economic system has, of course, received prolonged study, both theoretical and empirical, but without reaching a fully satisfactory explanation of how and why capital investment decisions are made.

This book is a study of a part of the subject, which arises out of the work of the Science and Industry Committee. The Committee was appointed by the Royal Society of Arts, by the British Association for the Advancement of Science, and by the Nuffield Foundation, to investigate factors influencing the rate of adoption of new scientific and technical ideas by British Industry. Our first report on these matters has been published;[1] but in the course of the investigations (which included case-studies in a considerable variety of firms) it was suggested by the Board of Trade that we might make a subsidiary report on 'material which would contribute to knowledge of the background of investment decisions'. The material which we can offer arises from a study of the application of new knowledge, that is of innovation, and it is true that this usually involves the creation of new kinds of capital goods, or of capital goods for new uses, and that therefore investment decisions must be taken. But many investment decisions are simply to extend or to duplicate capital goods already in use, and involve no element of innovation; this is why we only claim to cover a part of the subject.

The committee's methods are described in *Industry and Technical Progress*, and especially in Appendix II. Briefly, our evidence was

[1] C. F. Carter and B. R. Williams, *Industry and Technical Progress*, Oxford University Press, 1957.

derived from the study of some 250 firms, spread over most of the principal industries, and of various sizes, forms of ownership, and degrees of progressiveness. Not all of these yield useful information on investment decisions, but we have supplemented our knowledge by some special studies of the subject in selected firms and public corporations, and by relating our work to other material available in the literature of the subject. The committee gratefully acknowledges that the preparation of this book has been made possible by grants from the Board of Trade under the Conditional Aid scheme for the use of counterpart funds derived from United States economic aid. The committee, as well as its staff, has taken an active part in the work, but it deputed the writing of this book to us as its Directors of Research, leaving to us the detailed responsibility, and regarding its own function as being to make general suggestions, and finally to endorse the whole as worthy of publication.

The flow of investment in innovation will be large, and its results satisfactory, if there are many technical opportunities for such investment; if firms receive (and are ready to receive) an adequate stimulus to action; and if that action is not wasted through wrong decisions, or prevented by shortage of resources. In this complex group of factors the shortage of resources (especially as this is expressed in rates of interest) has attracted an undue share of notice. We do not question the ability of Governments to vary the ease with which resources can be obtained for investment, nor the fact that they do in fact make this variation; and we have tried (in Chapter Nine) to say something of what seems to us to be the relevance of rates of interest. But our main interest has been concentrated on the willingness to invest in innovation, and on the ability to invest effectively. Such matters as the extent of scientific education, the amount invested in research, the quality and effectiveness of the communication of new ideas, the willingness of firms to receive ideas from outside, and the pressure exerted by excess demand thus receive prominence. The decisions of firms are made on the basis of their expectations about a necessarily uncertain future, and we have studied the way in which these expectations are formed; in doing so, we have formed the opinion that the effects of uncertainty, frequently given a leading place in theoretical work on this subject, can easily be over-estimated.

In the final chapter we have tried to suggest some of the implications of our results for a Government which desires some control of investment as a means of encouraging economic growth while keeping to the narrow path between the devil of inflation and the deep seas of depression. After examining the complexity of the actions of firms, we are not surprised that investment in the 1950's has taken a course which has at times been an embarrassment to Government planners.

C. F. CARTER
B. R. WILLIAMS
Belfast and Keele,
April 1958

One Why study investment?

This book relates to a part of a large and variable element in national activity, the laws of whose determination and change are not known with any certainty. Capital investment in plant, machinery, and buildings is known to the economic statisticians as 'fixed investment', to distinguish it from investment in stocks of goods and work in progress. Fixed investment in 1957 amounted to nearly £3,400 m., or 18 per cent of the national product. This includes investment undertaken on Government and private account: about £1,500 m. was invested by Government (central and local) and the nationalized industries, and £1,900 m. by companies, partnerships and sole traders or private individuals. Over £1,200 m. was spent (by all sectors of the economy taken together) on plant and machinery, and of this about three-fifths was (notionally) replacement and two-fifths was a net addition to the stock of capital.

The spending of these large sums is vital to the maintenance and increase of output per head, and hence to a rising standard of living. Increases in output and the production of new kinds of goods are both closely related to the extension and improvement of capital equipment; and the improvement depends, not just on inventiveness, but on the willingness to incorporate new ideas and new knowledge in productive equipment. Hence the decision to 'invest in innovation' is a crucial one. The making of investment decisions is worth study on its own account, but it is also worth study because it is a component in the circuit which links the pure scientist in his laboratory to the consumer seeking a better satisfaction of his needs. Many people feel that this circuit shows an undue resistance to the passage and use of ideas, but the resistance might be at many points—a shortage of scientists, undue financial caution, poor selection of managers, and so on. In *Industry and Technical Progress* we have tried to examine the circuit as a whole, but we think that the present study, by concentrating attention on a particularly important component, may also help to show how to speed up the use of science in industry.

I

The spending on fixed investment is not necessarily determined by the same factors as determine the other main claimants on the national product—personal consumption, Government expenditure, and overseas investment. Furthermore, fixed investment is capable of big variations; thus, after being practically constant in real terms from 1950 to 1952, it rose by nearly 35 per cent in four years and by 11 per cent in one of these years (1952–3). The largest post-war year-to-year variation in real personal consumption was, by contrast, only 4½ per cent. On occasion private spending on particular goods can vary quite extensively, in response to actual or expected price changes or variations in Government restrictions; thus, expenditure on private vehicles rose (in real terms) by more than a half from 1952 to 1953. But correspondingly the variability of total investment hides a greater variability of its parts; thus, expenditure on road goods vehicles (which are included in 'fixed' investment) rose by 32 per cent from 1954 to 1955.

The potential output of the country varies only slowly from year to year; except in unusual circumstances, the main influence which alters it is the growth and improvement of capital equipment, itself the result of fixed investment. Large variations in the claims on the national product therefore set up considerable stresses. Some elasticity can be provided by variation in stocks, and perhaps by variations in imports and exports; but if most industrial capacity or labour is already fully employed, a sharp increase in one of the claims necessarily requires a cut for some of the other claimants. On the other hand, a sharp decrease may leave idle capacity, which for technical or economic reasons cannot be transferred to other uses, and which is thus wasted in idleness.

When there is an excess demand, to leave the claimants to fight things out among themselves will result in the competitive bidding-up of prices, and in the appearance of queues and delays in delivery. Hence comes the idea—which has been applied by all post-war Governments—that the State should by regulation or planning produce compensating variations in the claims, so that full employment of resources can be assured without inflation. But real life is not capable of such tidy regulation. Government expenditure, for instance, is quite largely for purposes on which long-term commitments have been made. Private individuals do not always do what gentlemen in Whitehall may desire, and in particular (because they hold money and bank balances) they need not at once adjust their expenditure to a change in income. Nor is capital investment itself easily regulated, for much of it is planned and executed over long periods, so that it is difficult and wasteful to alter it in mid-course.

Things are made more difficult by the long delays in obtaining information and in acting upon it. Changes in imports and exports are known fairly quickly, but a decided change in consumption or investment may not be known for certain to exist for two or three months after it has begun, and its size and importance may defy assessment for some time longer. The appropriate compensating action has then to be chosen and brought into effect; even in the most favourable circumstances, it may be many months before it brings results.

Thus Government action trails half a year or a year behind events, and—because so great a part of expenditure proves incapable of short-term control—the items which *can* be controlled tend to be subjected to violent change in the effort to provide the necessary compensating variation. It would appear to an outside observer, for instance, that this tends to happen to expenditure on roads, to the capital programmes of nationalized industries, and to expenditure on vehicles. To say that the Government should cease exercising a control which proves to be so crude and violent is no answer, for in its absence there would be the worse evils of greater inflation or of deflation. It is better to attempt, therefore, to find by patient study means of making the compensating variations less necessary, and (where they are required) of making them more accurate and timely.

A few years ago (in 1952) the Government appeared puzzled because the incentives it was offering for investment were not proving effective; three years later it was puzzled because it could not limit the flood of investment which had been let loose—though not necessarily as a result of the Government's policies. We suspect that it was this puzzlement which caused the Board of Trade to ask us to make our small contribution to an understanding of the process of investment. We would ask the reader, however, not to suppose that we have been studying the actions of business men in order that the Government may control them better. There is a larger purpose: a study of these actions, even where they are free and unrestrained, may help both the Government and the business community to foresee the time, direction, and extent of changes with greater accuracy, and thus to plan ahead with better results; and it may help towards a fuller and more speedy use of science in industry.

There has been some theorizing about investment decisions, but much of it has had little contact with reality. One complex element is the origin of opportunities to invest, and the way in which these opportunities impinge upon those with the power to make decisions; this is the first matter which we consider. Our observations on the reasons for making decisions to invest follow, but we have also given in the Appendix some of the more technical aspects of the theory of investment as it has been developed in the writings of economists. It can there be seen that the more recent theories have mostly assumed a precision of expectation, and an orderly rule of calculation, which would be hard indeed to find in the real world. We conclude our own study with a chapter which sets out some of the implications for Government policy of the ideas which we record. The investment decisions of the business community create an important and variable part of the national expenditure, and more knowledge about them is urgently needed. We therefore hope that our studies may stimulate further research.

Two The technical opportunity to invest

John Stuart Mill classified investment opportunities as those caused by waste, by inventions, by cheaper imports, and by broadening markets for capital. Various classifications of this kind can be made; and the relative importance of the causative factors varies from time to time and from place to place. When Adam Smith was writing, in the mid-eighteenth century, the chief place in promoting decisions to invest was held by the growth of markets; in the nineteenth century the opening up of new territories and the growth of population were together responsible for about half of the total volume of new capital formation, but other factors were growing in importance. In particular, invention was becoming very significant as a creator of investment opportunity in the western world; according to A. N. Whitehead, 'the greatest invention of the nineteenth century was the invention of the method of invention'. In our own time scientific discoveries provide the major opportunities for invention, and a scientific education is a precondition of practically all invention. The nature of the change can be seen from a brief examination of those great waves of economic growth in the eighteenth, nineteenth, and twentieth centuries which are often referred to as 'industrial revolutions'.

In the industrial revolution of the eighteenth century there was a group of inventions which mainly affected the textile and iron trades. The first of the inventions by which the textile industries were transformed was made in 1733 by John Kay, who was a weaver and reed-maker. By 1760 this invention, the flying shuttle, was in sufficiently general use to make worse a long-standing disequilibrium between spinning and weaving. Lewis Paul, with John Wyatt (a master carpenter), patented a spinning-machine in 1738. This machine, which was not sufficiently developed for successful use in production, seems to have been the basis of the water frame, believed to have been invented by Thomas Highs, a reed-maker, and John Kay the second, clockmaker of Warrington. It was patented in 1769 by Arkwright, who had been apprenticed to a barber and wig-maker and became a

5

dealer in hair.[1] Hargreaves, who combined the trades of weaver and carpenter, invented the spinning-jenny in or shortly before 1767. In 1779 Crompton, the son of a small farmer and weaver, invented the mule, which combined the principles of the jenny and the water frame and produced a strong fine cotton thread. The use of these inventions now caused weaving to lag behind spinning. The Reverend Edmund Cartwright, who was a Fellow of Magdalen College, Oxford—where his training in the classics and devotion to poetry were not a very obvious preparation for his later life as inventor and manufacturer—made the first step to the solution of this problem when in the 1780's he invented the power loom. However, this loom was not good enough for factory production, and the power loom was not much used in production for another thirty years, after substantial improvements by Horrocks, Radcliffe, and others.

The growth of the machine industry in textiles was dependent on developments in the metal industries. Here, too, there were great advances, made possible in the main by practical people who had no training in science. Because of the lack of charcoal the British iron industry was in a poor state. In the first decade of the eighteenth century, Abraham Darby the first, who began life as a millwright, discovered how to use coal as fuel by having it 'coked into cinder'. The problem was then to find a way of using coal not only to make pig-iron but also to refine it. This problem was solved by an improved process of puddling, simultaneously discovered by Onions, an iron-founder of Merthyr Tydvil, and Cort—described by Watt as 'a simple good natured man, but not very knowing'. This process, discovered by entirely empirical methods, was substantially modified in the nineteenth century, when developments in chemistry made possible a scientific explanation of the process of decarbonization.

In both the metal and textile industries modern techniques are thus based on inventions made by men with practically no theoretical knowledge. With Watt's steam-engine (1765) scientific method made its first important appearance. Newcomen, a blacksmith and locksmith, invented his steam pump in 1705; after a number of improvements by others, it was a useful engine. James Watt, a scientific-instrument maker, attended Black's lectures at Glasgow on the theory of latent heat, and conducted a series of experiments on the pressure of steam. When, therefore, in 1764 he studied the mechanism of a Newcomen engine used in the practical physics course at

[1] See P. Mantoux, *The Industrial Revolution in the Eighteenth Century,* Jonathan Cape, 1928, pp. 208–34.

Glasgow, he was able to explain the reasons for its loss of energy and to deduce the means by which the energy loss could be remedied. It is not unreasonable to say that Watt's invention was worked out in a laboratory by scientific methods. Its application to industry was on a small scale until well into the nineteenth century, but we can see in this eighteenth-century development a process of invention that has now become dominant.

The second period of change, from the 1840's to the end of the century, was based on steam and steel. Some of the decisive inventions were made earlier, but for economic growth it is the application that matters, and that often takes place a considerable time after the key invention. Frequently the application of an invention will in itself involve further invention. This was so, for example, in the use of steam power for transport. The railway engine and the steamship were developed in the first half of the nineteenth century by 'practical engineers' such as Stephenson.

The developments of steel production in Britain were made possible by Bessemer, Siemens, and Thomas. Henry Bessemer has been described as 'more an inventor than a scientist'.[1] Certainly he had no scientific education, and the elements of his major 'invention'—the Bessemer method of steel making—were not scientific novelties. However, he seems to have acquired a good deal of chemical knowledge; with this and his great practical experience he combined known devices—such as the use of air blast and of added manganese —and overcame the obstacles to their use to produce cheap steel. William Siemens, who in the 1860's invented the open-hearth process of making steel, did possess considerable scientific knowledge. His work on steel arose out of his invention of the regenerative gas furnace, which itself grew out of his theoretical studies of heat economy. Sidney Gilchrist Thomas became a police-court clerk at the age of seventeen, and began at home to experiment and to study the unsolved problems of chemistry. From the time when he heard Chaloner, in a course of evening lectures given at the Birkbeck Institute in 1870, say that 'the man who eliminates phosphorus by means of the Bessemer converter would make his fortune', he sought the secret of the dephosphorization of iron in the converter.[2] This, with the help of his cousin who was a chemist in a Welsh ironworks, he discovered in 1878, and his process of giving the converter a basic lining was very quickly adopted, for it made possible the use of

[1] Jewkes, Sawers, and Stillerman, *The Sources of Invention*, Macmillan, 1958, p. 52.
[2] *Memoir and Letters of Gilchrist Thomas*, John Murray, 1891.

British phosphoric ores. These changes in the steel industry affected practically all productive processes; in particular, they made possible improvements in steam-driven machinery and in machine tools, and facilitated that increase in accuracy which made mass production possible.

The inventions in steel-making took place in a different way from the earlier discoveries in textile machinery. The scientists had a part to play as well as the 'practical men'. The opportunity for acquiring scientific knowledge from books and journals or from other scientists was steadily increasing. It is thus not surprising that the next big changes in industry—starting from the turn of the century—were in part due to scientific developments in chemistry and electrical engineering. The chemical industry existed before the great development of chemical theory of the 1860's—there was considerable manufacture of various alkalis and acids and refining of metals. By the middle of the nineteenth century the majority of the processes of manufacture could be explained in terms of chemical reactions.[1] At that time, however, organic chemistry was chaotic and the organic chemical industry did not exist. Its growth, bringing the manufacture of dyes, drugs, explosives, and plastics, was not only spectacular but also very different from that of the inorganic chemical industry. The manufacture of organic chemicals not only required chemists to start it off, but also to supervise it. That is why Germany, which had very little chemical industry in the 1840's but was becoming preeminent in the theory and teaching of chemistry, became the leader in the organic chemical industry and then in the application of the principles of physical chemistry to inorganic processes.[2] The manufacture of artificial silk did develop in Britain, but otherwise Britain failed to use the industrial potential of organic chemistry until after the First World War. This failure to use the technical opportunity to invest—largely because very few industrial chemists were being trained—helps to explain why the growth of British output per head fell behind that of Germany.

The manufacture of organic chemicals was based on scientific discoveries. In electricity theoretical developments took place a long time before practical applications were envisaged. The basis of the

[1] See Sherwood Taylor, *A History of Industrial Chemistry*, Heinemann, 1957.

[2] For the organization of science in Britain in the nineteenth century, see D. S. L. Cardwell, *The Organization of Science in England, A retrospect*, Heinemann, 1957. For a brief description of the growth of the organic chemical industry, see Sherwood Taylor, op. cit., chapters 17 and 18.

electrical industry was the discovery of the electric current (1780) and of the Voltaic cell needed to produce it (1799). In 1831 Faraday discovered the possibility of generating electricity by moving a conductor in a magnetic field. From this point it was a relatively small step to the use of electricity for telegraphy, light, and power. Many magneto-electric machines were built, but it was half a century later that workers such as the American inventor Thomas Edison (who in the 1870's had an industrial research laboratory employing 100 men[1]) produced a really efficient generator. The first electric-light bulbs were developed by Edison and Swan (a spare-time scientist), who both knew in advance the form of the solution, but had to find a way to evacuate the bulb and to make a filament of high resistance. These developments created the electrical-engineering industry, and prepared for the development of electronics and of atomic energy.

The industrial development of the chemical and electrical industries from the end of the century, with its flow of invention and innovation, was based on scientific knowledge. A scientific education was becoming essential for the inventor; by the end of the First World War the dependence of invention on the supply of trained chemists and physicists, and on the supply of money to finance expensive research and development in universities and industrial laboratories, was widely recognized.

The development of the internal-combustion engine, another source of recent changes in industry, was based on discoveries in chemistry and physics which produced better metals, and on a knowledge of the properties of electricity. Otherwise the earlier developments were largely empirical; many of the inventors and innovators were mechanics and not scientists. As the internal-combustion engine increased in power, however, this ceased to be so. An interesting illustration of this is provided by the career of the inventor of the Whittle jet-propulsion gas turbine. Whittle, as an Air Force cadet, received a training in science subjects, including mechanics and the theory of flight. He then took an Officers' Engineering Course, and after this was sent to the University of Cambridge to take the Mechanical Sciences Tripos. He had conceived the idea of the jet engine before he went to Cambridge, but it was after his university course that Whittle successfully developed his engine. The development required very exacting research, design, and development work on the part of Whittle and his team, as well as research and development work on the part of firms which agreed to supply

[1] J. D. Bernal, *Science and Industry in the Nineteenth Century*, Routledge, 1953.

components or alloys for the engine. Thus, to give one important example, Firth Vickers developed a new nickel–chrome alloy to avoid failure in the turbine blades.[1]

The change in the inventive process during the last two hundred years is not surprising. In the eighteenth century the body of scientific knowledge was small and there was little scientific activity. Since then the amount of scientific effort and knowledge has grown enormously. This has taken place because of changed attitudes to education and in particular to scientific education,[2] and because of growing wealth, which has made possible an increasing expenditure on education, research, and development. As the result of these changes, invention is now often the result of a planned and co-operative research and development programme. Because there is a large body of background scientific knowledge, it is often reasonable to say, after a study of the relevant literature, that a particular problem can in principle be solved. The next step may be to plan a research programme, and because of the fine specialization in training it may be necessary or advisable to include in a research team scientists from different disciplines. Such group activity has been used extensively in research and development for atomic energy, and it is quite common in many other types of research in chemistry and physics. In mechanical engineering and similar fields individual activity is still predominant, though the chance of a significant invention by an *amateur* is now small. By 'amateur' is meant a person without any technical training at all; inventions are, of course, sometimes made by people with a scientific or engineering training in some other field. The importance of cross fertilization in scientific discovery and invention is well known; so, too, is the importance of the fresh (but trained) mind. But although these two factors may enable isolated individuals to make discoveries, they may have a stronger influence in making possible discoveries by team effort.

When we are concerned with development rather than research the importance of the group becomes greater. To scale up a process from laboratory size, or to judge the wisdom of trying one form of production rather than another, frequently requires the work of a design and development team. This happens sometimes because the development process needs to take into account the problems and interests of the production and sales departments. The more fundamental reason, however, is that scientific and engineering advance

[1] Sir Frank Whittle, *Jet*, Muller, 1953 (Pan Books, 1957).
[2] See, e.g., Cardwell, op. cit.

has entailed a growing division of labour, and work based on division of labour requires extensive organization.

'The opportunity to invest' could be taken as including the economic conditions which make investment possible and worth while; but these economic forces are dealt with in later chapters, and we are here concerned with 'technical opportunity'—that is to say, with the existence in a suitably developed form of processes and products which could be adopted by a manufacturer. How are these opportunities made known to the firm—whether as minor improvements for use in the replacement or replication of capital assets, or as major projects for mainly or entirely new work, involving perhaps entire new industrial plants?

It is seldom that opportunities for investment arise simply from the appearance in the Managing Director's office of an independent inventor with an idea for sale.[1] Many *Punch* cartoons have featured the inventor, patiently queuing at the Patent Office with his mysterious parcel, and it is, of course, true that some ingenious individuals devote their spare time to the invention of products of a small and miscellaneous kind. Such people are often devoid of much commercial sense, and are unable to make headway unless they can interest an established manufacturer; and they sometimes find it difficult to believe that what seems to them to be technically so excellent is not worth commercial exploitation.

Nor do opportunities of investment often arise *directly* from the institutes of pure science, in the universities and elsewhere. The emphasis here is on 'directly'; the work of the pure scientist is, of course, not only considered valuable as an addition to knowledge, but is often of the greatest indirect importance to industry. But a large gap separates the proving of an idea in theory, or on a laboratory scale, and its development to the point of commercial exploitation. The bridging of this gap may be much more expensive than the original research, and a large number of apparently promising projects are necessarily rejected at the development stage. The university scientist, like the inventor, sometimes finds it tiresome that a useful product, or a process seemingly ripe for industrial application, should nevertheless not be developed, or find its development only after great delay; but many things other than technical quality have to be taken into account in making the decision to invest money in commercial exploitation.

The nursery-grounds where we must look for technical opportuni-

[1] See *Industry and Technical Progress*, Chapters 3 and 5.

ties of investment, well grown and ready for planting out, are therefore the research and development department of the firm itself, or
the sales departments of supplying firms, or (in rarer but significant
cases) the buying departments of customer firms; or occasionally
institutions which (like some research associations) conduct applied
research *to the point of commercial usefulness*, or which (like the National
Research Development Corporation) introduce discoveries made by
Government bodies to a wider circle of users.

For a particular firm, most of the investment opportunities may
come from outside; indeed, the firm's resources may be too small to
enable it to develop for itself anything more than minor improvements to products and processes. But the process of development
must have taken place somewhere. If it has occurred in a supplying
firm—for instance, a supplier of a new machine—that firm must itself have invested what may be a large amount in developing the
machine, and in the capacity necessary to produce it. It has made
this investment in anticipation of the demand for the machine, and
its effectiveness in creating investment opportunities in the firms
which it supplies depends on its skill in judging the demand—that is
to say, on its market research and salesmanship. The firm must also
be skilful in judging whether the outcome of its scientific or technical
research is likely to be within the compass of its financial and
managerial capacity to sustain development and production. The
development may turn out to have been misdirected; and, of course,
misdirected development *within* a firm may also fail to create the investment opportunities which are desired. This is a reminder, therefore, that there are two main elements in the creation of investment
opportunities: the allocation of resources to research and development and the direction of these resources in a well-judged and skilful
manner.

Given reasonable skill and judgement, it is very broadly true that
the more resources you devote to research and development, the
more results you will get out. Earth-shaking discoveries cannot, of
course, be laid on to order, but most new products and processes
evolve by small steps, the speed of evolution depending on the number of good minds and the amount of technical facilities available.
Research and development is an investment in progress; from the
point of view we are now taking, it is an *investment in the creation of
opportunities of further investment*. It is therefore highly significant that
industrial research and development expenditure in the United
Kingdom has been on a swiftly rising curve, similar to (though later

than) the curve for the United States, and that the rise in both countries is apparently continuing. It is significant because it marks the change from a world in which new technical opportunities of investment came by chance at irregular intervals to one in which they are the result of a prior decision to devote resources to development.

Research and development expenditure in the United States has, even after adjustment for price changes, multiplied itself by a factor of at least twenty since the First World War. The scattered data for the United Kingdom show a swift and recent rise, to a level roughly equal to that for the United States when measured as a proportion of the gross national product, though the absolute amount spent remains, of course, much lower. But in Britain an unusually high proportion of the expenditure has been undertaken by or financed by Government agencies, so that there is a strong bias towards defence purposes and atomic research; the United States must be presumed to be still well in the lead in the proportion of income devoted to research for direct civilian purposes. In both countries there are large differences in research effort according to industry. The intensity of research effort can be measured in many ways—in relation to net output, or to number employed, or to turnover, or profits, or investment. Our inquiries confirm that, however it is measured, there is great variation in this intensity, even between firms of similar size and in apparently similar industries. An extreme example is provided by the aircraft industry, a large part of whose expenditure can be classed as research, design, or development.

The differences are in part explained by the differences in the contributions made to defence. Apart from this, the greatest attention is given to research and development where there is a developed science or technology with a direct bearing on the industry's products or processes. Such an industry has a store of 'back-ground knowledge' on which it can draw, and it can usually find a supply of scientists trained in the appropriate fields. The opportunity of profitably using scientists for research and development is therefore more obvious than in traditional industries. Scientific advance is likely to have an immediate effect on the investment opportunities of firms in the industry; failure to seize the opportunities may lead to bankruptcy.

The rate of creation of investment opportunities in different industries is not, of course, necessarily proportional to their direct research and development expenditures. Some industries are parasitic on others for their ideas, and some developments are capable of application far outside the boundaries of the industries which created them. In each industry tradition is important, and so is the supply of first-rate trained minds and the extent of co-operation for training and research. An industry with the habit of co-operation, with a respect for what can be achieved by research, and with a good supply of scientists, technologists, and managers, may create wide investment opportunities with no very high research expenditure. But we must not forget also the chance element—the fact that at a particular place and time developments in many fields are ready to converge, and to create from their convergence an explosion of new possibilities. Such occasions provide the great exceptions to the rule that the output of usable results is in broad relation to the scale of resources used to get them.

The increase in British research and development expenditure is considerable, but it is recent; and this means that the flow of technical investment opportunities is likely to increase, not only with the rising development expenditure, but also with the increasing usefulness of research, which in its infancy must often start far back from the point of application. An industry with a new interest in science often has to begin with fundamental research on the properties of its materials; some immediate practical benefit is obtained from the work of the scientists in 'trouble-shooting' or in elementary operational research, but it may be a decade or even more before substantial results, developed to the point of commercial application, begin to emerge. Hence it is to be expected that the flow of investment opportunities, though slow at first, will later increase. In a backward industry or country people complain of the shortage of ideas; but in an advanced scientific country the point may be reached when an increase of investment in the creation and development of ideas is not worth while, because they are queuing up faster than resources can be found to employ them.

It is worth remembering that the investment opportunities open to a particular firm include any that it can obtain or adapt from the experience of others—so far as patents and other restrictions allow, from the best experience it can find anywhere in the world. Since firms are of variable quality and differing past history, this means that the opportunities currently open include not only the ideas coming from the development department, and those being pressed upon the firm by its suppliers or demanded by its customers, but also a whole stock of opportunities discovered elsewhere and so far left unexploited by the firm. The technical opportunity may be a matter of common knowledge for many years (as in the application of diesel traction to British Railways), but it has to wait for other favourable circumstances before it can go through the final stages of development and application. Even so, however, the diesel train represents the results of the decisions to develop of various firms and bodies, taken in other countries and many years ago; its use is still linked, though by a long chain, to the decision to commit resources to research and development which we here suggest to be the prime mover in the creation of investment opportunities.

It must be remembered that our discussion of the creation of investment opportunities relates to innovation, and not to the whole of investment. The relative importance of innovation is not easy to assess in statistical terms. Of the gross total of fixed investment, nearly £3,400 m. in 1957, about three-fifths was in theory used to replace assets which had worn out. But the concept of 'replacement' is a difficult one. It is seldom easy to measure the degree of wear of a machine or a building, or to decide to what extent it has ceased to be able to perform its desired function. Often it is the function which has changed, rather than the machine, and the problem is one of deciding what degree of obsolescence is tolerable. If one sets onself to answer the question 'what proportion of the nation's stock of houses is due for replacement next year?', it is clear that the answer is bound to be arbitrary. In a particular year it is possible to replace no houses at all, tolerating disrepair and out-of-date standards for a little longer; over a period of years some replacement is obviously necessary, but it could be based with almost equal plausibility on an assumed life of sixty years or on one of 150 years. Nor is this the end of the problem, for houses pulled down will certainly be replaced by quite different kinds of houses, embodying new standards and new techniques, and probably costing more than their predecessors, even after allowing for changes in prices. It will be almost impossible to say what proportion of the price is attributable to improvements; indeed, some of the features of the house replaced, such as an earth closet, may have no present-day price.

Replacement is so to speak, the routine side of investment; and our evidence relates to the introduction of new products and new processes, which might seem to be a separate part of investment. The argument of the last paragraph, however, shows that it is not possible to separate pure replacement from pure innovation; they are inextricably confused. The example taken from housing can be paralleled from machinery, vehicles, or factory buildings. Every car owner knows the problems of deciding when an old car is due for re-placement; and he knows, too, that it will usually be replaced by a car which embodies the technical progress of the intervening years.

Of the new investment, some involves no more than a reproduc-tion of capital assets already existing—the doubling of the capacity of a factory, an addition to a fleet of ships or aircraft. But, again, such pure replication is not very common; usually the latest addition contains to some extent the results of technical progress over the period since the previous model was built, or the modifications sug-gested by experience with earlier models.

The 'innovation component' is perhaps not very great in building, which accounts for nearly half of the gross total of investment; though even in building new materials and techniques have had an important influence—for instance, pre-stressed concrete, pre-fabri-cation and the use of the tower crane, laminated plastics, new floor-ing materials, and so on. About 15 per cent of investment takes the form of vehicles, ships, and aircraft, and here the effects of innova-tion are more obvious, especially in the aircraft and road vehicle fields. In plant and machinery, over a third of the total of investment, there are certain massive items which appear essentially 'traditional' —for instance, conventional power stations, iron and steel works, and machinery for the cotton and wool trades, for the food trades, or for the older types of engineering. But even these have been pro-foundly influenced by such things as new materials, new methods of control, new cutting speeds for tools, new handling devices; the changes are to be seen in such measures as the rising efficiency of electricity generation. Substantial investment in plant and machin-ery is also required for the chemical and pharmaceutical trades, oil refining, man-made fibres, aircraft, atomic energy, and electrical engineering—all trades in which the rate of innovation of both pro-duct and process tends to be high. Thus, although it is impossible to give a meaningful answer to a question about the exact size of the 'innovation component' in investment, that component is certainly substantial. Two centuries ago, most of the products and processes in everyday use had existed with little change for hundreds of years; today we are surrounded by products and processes which were un-known when the century began.

Three The problem of uncertainty

It is quite clear that there is in most important investment decisions an irreducible uncertainty. By this we do not mean a *risk* capable of statistical assessment on the basis of past observation; for such risks can usually be in large measure offset by insurance. Nor do we mean merely a lack of that knowledge which the prudent business man might be expected to be able to acquire; it is true that in our observation some investment decisions are taken without a proper and possible assessment of technical problems or of markets, but the willingness of some managers to proceed, like foolish virgins, without taking care to light their way, constitutes a separate problem. What we seek to discuss in this chapter is the problem of navigation in the fog which normally and inevitably surrounds the future.

The density of that fog must not be under-estimated. We have had access to data about the relation between expectation and performance in a number of investment decisions. It is remarkable how frequently and extensively market conditions have changed in the period between the making of a decision and its execution. In consequence, new processes installed for product A are, before they are ever worked, converted to make product B; plant installed to meet an apparently inevitable rise in demand remains idle because that demand has suddenly receded; the profitability of a process is violently changed by some change in relative prices; a process 'proven' in the United States turns out to need much change to suit British conditions. We have the impression that in industries subject to rapid technical change or unstable market conditions such large differences between expectation and realized performance for particular projects must be regarded as normal, and that the best which a manager can hope to achieve is to be somewhere near right on the average of a series of decisions.

In these industries, and in others apparently more stable, large changes in conditions may be brought about by unforeseen Government action, by political events abroad, or even by the hazards of the weather or the whims of fashion. A manufacturer of electronic components for use in guided missiles cannot be expected to foresee the changes of the defence programme. A motor manufacturer must invest very heavily in the dies and tools required for the current styling of his car bodies, but a change of fashion may make his chosen style look archaic. A plant for producing a synthetic material may be rendered suddenly useless by a change in the price of a competing natural material, such as may be caused by a bumper crop. Indeed, the possible uncertainties are so great that it is at first sight surprising that 'enterprises of great pitch and moment' are ever carried out.

We have already made the distinction between statistically assessable risks and the irreducible uncertainty of the unknown future. But this distinction is not a sharp one. There are insurable risks (e.g. arising in atomic plants) for which the record of past disaster is not sufficient to give a sound foundation for statistical assessment. There are non-insurable risks which can nevertheless be to some extent weighed and measured with the help of past occurrences which were *similar but not identical*. There are, of course, some business decisions which are unique in the sense that no past full-scale experience throws any light whatever on their chances of success—they involve a process or product which is radically new, and whose prospects can only be judged from theory or from laboratory experiment. But it is much more usual for there to be some evidence from ventures which embody similar principles. Consider, for instance, the first decision to use main-line diesel-electric locomotives on British Railways. This was a technical innovation involving a considerable investment. Apart from information which could be obtained from trials, there was much available information about the operation of such locomotives in other countries—though no doubt under conditions of use, load, climate, fuel and labour costs, and maintenance arrangements which would never be exactly paralleled in Britain. The irreducible uncertainty in such a case relates to the effect of the divergence of British from foreign conditions, and to the future changes in British conditions—the trends of railway rates and traffics, of the taxation of road users, and so on. The big issue was probably the intensity of use of the locomotives—whether it would be possible, now and in the future, to arrange their schedules so as to obtain an adequate number of ton-miles of haulage per year while still assuring reliability by adequate maintenance. Obviously, in the absence of any information from other countries, the uncertainty would have been much greater; and it is an important objective of an efficient management to reduce uncertainty by getting this relevant, but not exactly applicable, information.

Another distinction which has to be made is between the human and the physical uncertainties. The human uncertainties include such things as the reactions of competitors, the policies of Governments, and the attitudes of labour to innovation. The physical uncertainties are (for instance) whether some new snags will appear in the transition from a laboratory model or a pilot plant to full-scale production, or whether the product will have the properties expected of it. The physical uncertainties are in general capable of reduction (though not necessarily of elimination) by scientific study and research, though the cost of trying to overcome snags in advance may not be worth while—at some point it may be best to 'take a risk' and hope that all will turn out well. The physical uncertainties are clearly very much less in the replacement or replication of existing plant, perhaps with minor modification, than in the adoption of an entirely new process or product. When the element of innovation is negligible, the physical uncertainty may be negligible also; the belief that one's new car will show certain operating characteristics is solidly based on the observation of exactly similar cars already in use.

But the human uncertainties are a much more serious matter. Where they depend on the simple reactions of large numbers—e.g. the opinions of numerous housewives about a new detergent—they may be capable of assessment by statistical techniques. We have mentioned in *Industry and Technical Progress*[1] our view that some British industries do not make sufficient use of market research; they thus suffer from a removable uncertainty. But more complex reactions, and the reactions of one man or of small groups of men, are much more difficult to foresee. At this point the lessening of uncertainty becomes an art rather than a science, and involves an imaginative understanding of human nature. Even this will not go far, if the uncertainty is a side-effect of a decision in some quite different field; thus, the imaginative business man may be able to guess, with some success, the reactions of his work-people or of his competitors to his own actions, but he is not in a good position to judge whether a politician in a distant land will introduce a large disturbing influence by a decision to impose stringent import restrictions, or even to make war.

Yet another way of analysing uncertainty, and one which perhaps comes close to the mental processes which people in fact use in trying

I.I.I.—2   [1] p. 161.

to deal with the problem, is to draw a line of division between future states and their effects. To each investment decision there will correspond a *time-horizon*, that is to say, a point in future time which is 'as far ahead as one looks' in thinking of the particular investment. The time-horizon is obviously likely to be related to the expected life of the plant involved, though it may be shorter than that life. Given a time-horizon, there will be a great many possible events occurring within that time-horizon which will affect the outcome of the decision. Thus there may be peace, or war next year, or war the year after: a Conservative Government or a Labour Government: an American slump next year, or a boom; an extension of free trade or a heightening of trade barriers. These possible events or states will not all be taken into consideration, for they will usually be very numerous, some will appear highly improbable, and others will seem too insignificant in their likely effects on the outcome of the decision. There is thus a series of judgements about the extent to which these future states should be taken into consideration, the judgements being jointly affected by the likelihood of occurrence of the states and the importance of their effects. There may, however, be a tendency to leave out of account possibilities involving very large and wholly unknown effects; thus, a nuclear war which would wipe out half the population is certainly not impossible, but most business men (and private individuals) act as though the possibility did not exist.

Thus by a process of selection a small number of future states is retained for active consideration, and thereby the problem of uncertainty is reduced to a more manageable size. The possible investment decisions (to build or not to built this plant, to make that machine 'single-purpose' or adaptable) can then be considered in relation to these states or events chosen for consideration. It is possible that a particular decision then appears best 'whatever happens', or best except on the occurrence of a minority of the less likely future possibilities. Decision will then be easy; but in other cases one course may be best in certain future states, and quite a different course in other states which are equally (or almost equally) likely. The difficulty of decision may then be avoided by delay—in the hope for instance, that it will be easier to see the right thing to do after the next General Election; or the difficulty may be resolved by finding a further course of action with advantages 'whatever happens', as may happen if a difficulty in foreseeing future demand leads to the purchase of a machine with a widely adaptable range of output. Or again it may be possible to back two or more horses to win—to divide the decision, as when a Stock Exchange investor 'hedges' by buying a 'portfolio' of shares, some of which will do well in situation A, and others in situation B. Or action may be limited to projects which, under present conditions, will pay for themselves in a very short time. Or finally there may be that kind of irreducible uncertainty which can only be resolved by tossing a penny, calling in the astrologers, or following some personal whim or fancy.

This description of the way in which decisions are made in face of uncertainty is put forward as being reasonable and in accord with common-sense expectations; and some parts of it can be tested by observation, particularly of financial or Stock Exchange investment. It is not, however, directly derived from a study of ordinary business decisions. This is because it is difficult to observe mental attitudes to uncertainty; one must start with the realized fact—the decision actually taken—and it is not easy to go behind this to bring in all the alternative courses of action which were, or could have been, considered. Indeed, if a decision is taken by a committee, it may have commended itself for different reasons to different people. We give later, however, in Chapter Seven, some conclusions which we have been able to reach from our case-studies about business attitudes to uncertainty.

But if the description has any substance, it may serve to draw attention to some important points. The first of these is the difference between the uncertainty relating to general future states—war and peace, boom and slump, one or another kind of Government—and the uncertainty relating to the outcome of an investment *in* those states. The first the firm must tackle as best it can, by seeking a good and well-informed judgement on the progress of events; it can seldom hope to influence those events. The uncertainty about the outcome of a particular investment, under particular future circumstances, may be capable of being removed or lessened—for instance, by preparatory design and development work and by a careful survey of market conditions.

The second point is that uncertainty may not only affect the acceptance or rejection of a proposal to invest; it may lead to a modification of the proposal, to an adaptation to varying possibilities, or to 'hedging'. The third point is that the judgements, both of future events and of their effects, are essentially personal; and this directs our attention to the personalities who actually make these judgements, their background, and their habits of mind. Any theory of investment which depends on a machine-like reaction to external stimuli is likely to depart far from the truth; the reality has about it the untidiness and unpredictability of humanity.

We have stressed earlier in this chapter the density of the fog which surrounds the future. In our observation, however, it would be a mistake to suppose that all investment decisions are darkened by the consciousness of uncertainty. On the contrary, at certain times many business men proceed with their work of installing plant, building factories, and bringing out new products with as much confidence as though the future were certain. Our analysis above suggests several reasons why this may be so. It may be that the same course of investment is prudent, whatever the future circumstances—as when people say, 'We cannot go wrong if we do this.' It may be that the investment is forced upon the firm by the breakdown of existing plant or by the actions of its competitors. It may be that those who have to make the decision have so simplified the problem, by ignoring what they consider less likely, that they have made the outcome appear obvious. It may be that they are affected by some high fever of optimism, which encourages them to treat favourable possibilities as though they were certainties. There is no doubt of the tendency of optimism to spread like a contagious fever, so that at certain times most people feel sure that they are in a period of great expansion and rapid change, when decisions must be quick and bold; equally, at certain times the cold touch of pessimism is felt, and people look nervously about them, unwilling to be the first to make a move. It happens that many of our case-studies were made in a period of optimism, and our results must be interpreted with this in mind.

It might seem that a firm which is quick in adopting new scientific and technical ideas would be more affected by uncertainty than a firm which goes on in much the same way from year to year. But in fact the opposite is often true. The progressive firm has more risky changes to make, but it is also much more likely to analyse its investment problems in a scientific manner, and to gather up all the data about techniques, markets, supplies of materials, and so forth which may help it to reach a decision. In contrast, the less-progressive firm is likely to be backward not only in industrial techniques but also in the tools of management; it may have fewer decisions to make, but they are made in the dark. There is also the class of firms which are unprogressive because of the great uncertainty of their trade—obsessed by the state of their current order book, they are never able to take the long views needed in major technical advance. These firms make no investment in innovations, because the future always seems too uncertain; they have been defeated by uncertainty, whereas some of the leaders in technical progress have faced uncertainty and, to their own satisfaction, have overcome it.

A special case of the problem of uncertainty is to be found in the nationalized industries, such as coal, electricity, and rail transport. Most of these industries have a high ratio of capital to output, so that their investment is especially large and important. Their investment decisions have three notable features. First, a single body holds under its control the investment planning for a major product or service which is essential to other industries. If serious dislocation is to be avoided, the investment planning has to be on a grand scale, looking forward for many years into the future. Second, the annual execution of investment plans is subject to a Government control which is more direct than the control normally exercised over private industry. Third, the nationalized undertakings are very large, and the translation of an overall investment plan into actual projects undertaken at a local level involves difficult problems of co-ordination. The first and third of these features are shared by certain large and important undertakings in private industry, but the difficulties and uncertainties are seen in a clear and extreme form in the nationalized industries. Our inquiries about them have related to general investment planning; we have not pursued our investigations to cover particular schemes of investment in innovation.

The National Coal Board publishes its long-term investment plans from time to time. The 'Plan for Coal' in 1950 envisaged a demand for 230–280 m. tons of coal by 1961–5, and contemplated the expenditure of £635 m. (at 1949 prices), over fifteen years, to achieve this output. Much of this was expenditure to replace worked-out or inefficient mines, but there was a significant element of innovation in the plans for coal-getting, mine transport, and surface treatment. In 1955 a new plan, 'Investment in Coal', contemplated an investment of £1,350 m. over the period 1950–65 to obtain 240 m. tons by 1965, and it looked forward to 250 m. tons by 1970. The main factor in this revision was a fuller realization of the costs of new capacity, and of the diminishing returns to capital caused by deeper mines and narrower seams. The limits to the speed of development have been set by real shortages, especially of mining engineers, rather than by finance; up to 1957 it was broadly assumed that it was essential to win every possible ton of coal, but the recession of early 1958 produced a questioning of this attitude.

Since it may take up to ten years to get a major colliery working at full pressure, it is necessary for the National Coal Board to look a long way ahead in its planning; but the demand for coal even ten years hence is difficult to foresee, partly because it depends on assumptions about future industrial production and about prices, and now partly because of the uncertainty of the rate of development of nuclear power. Even after a figure of desired output has been estimated, the experience of recent years suggests that it is difficult to assess what level of capital expenditure is necessary to attain this output.

Similarly in the electricity supply industry there have been several estimates of future demand for electricity, of future increases of generating capacity, and of the cost of creating that capacity. Demand estimation in this case appears to be greatly influenced by the extrapolation of past trends; the industry has grown fast for a long time, the end to this growth is not in sight, and reliance on the trend is perhaps as good as the hazardous estimation of the future requirements of particular consumers. Nevertheless, the growth of demand depends on price policy, and the industry has come in for strong criticism of the assumptions and the detailed structure of its prices. The estimation of the cost of conventional generating capacity is no doubt much easier than the estimation of the cost of mining coal in uncertain geological conditions; but there must be great uncertainty about cost if nuclear power stations are taken into account.

When a nationalized industry produces a plan for investment, therefore, the apparent precision of the figures it contains will probably conceal considerable uncertainty about the physical objectives being sought, and about the resources necessary to attain them. This might not matter so much if the industry was then free to modify its use of resources from year to year as better information became available. But in fact the year-to-year modifications are frequently made by the Government on grounds of general economic policy having no direct connexion with the industry concerned. Since the public corporations are not expected, on an average of years, to make a profit, they are not normally in a position to finance much of their expansion or innovation by ploughing back their own profits; they therefore lack that independence of action which is possible for ordinary companies, even in times of credit restriction, provided that they are making profits. Nor is it sufficient that the public corporations should be given free access to the capital market, to borrow their requirements at whatever price the market sets. In practice, the public corporations are large borrowers at fixed interest, competing as borrowers with the Government itself, and they cannot be left to borrow as they wish. Therefore during much of the post-war period the annual execution of investment plans has been subject to variation in accordance with the Treasury's policy; and the reports of the corporations are full of references to the limitations within which they have had to work:

It was mentioned in the Second Annual Report that after the devaluation of sterling in the autumn of 1949 the Commission had been notified that severe restrictions on capital investment would be imposed. Representations were immediately made regarding the serious consequences which reductions might have upon the efficiency of the railways. Nevertheless, a cut of some 8 per cent in the stated reuqirements was imposed, although a concession was obtained that the reduction should be effected in stages, the lower annual rate being achieved by the end of the year. (Transport, 1950 report.)

Whilst the under-spending during 1951 was mainly due to physical shortages, in previous years it was chiefly the restrictions on expenditure which made it impossible to overtake all the accrued arrears of maintenance and renewal, or to put in hand many planned works of improvement and development which would have facilitated traffic, secured economies in operation and strengthened the earning power of the undertaking. (Transport, 1951 report.)

The 1954 report refers to a minor first beginning with new development, and to the hopes associated with the railway modernization plan. It is so far uncertain how far the 1957 'cuts' will have affected this plan, and (by delaying the time when the railways can offer a good service) will have caused a disappointment of the hopes of the plan's originators. It is at least known that the upward movement of expenditure will be slowed down, and the period of the plan extended.[1]

In 1951 the Central Electricity Authority made representations following statements in the 1951 Economic Survey about investment cuts. ('It will be necessary to reduce the total programmes of civil investment for 1951 and 1952 in order to make room for further defence building work. These are being re-examined, and until the examination is completed it is impossible to say how large the cuts in civil investment will be, or where they will fall.') The 1951–2 report refers to the final decision in August 1951: 'The Government first proposed a severe cut in distribution capital investment; but when

---

[1] Since these words were written, a renewed acceleration of modernization has been permitted—this time as part of a wages settlement.

it became clear that this would have delayed the provision of supplies to new housing estates of local authorities, the proposed allocation was increased to meet the minimum requirements of the Area Boards.' In other words, this allocation was decided not in relation to any economically desirable long-term plan of the electricity industry, but as a by-product of a priority given to local-authority housing. In the earlier post-war years Government control of investment in electricity was exercised by controlling actual physical programmes, but from 1953 a mainly financial control has been used; thus for 1956–7 the Government requested a curtailment of capital development, though not of power-station construction, and the programme was cut first from £213 m. to £204 m., and then to £195 m.; at this level the Authority stated that they would in fact have to postpone construction work on some power stations. Actual expenditure turned out to be £206 m. ('which under the circumstances, the Minister approved') because work went ahead faster than expected; so in this case the attempt at control was ineffective.

Clearly the nationalized industries cannot be allowed to do just as they like, any more than private industry is allowed to act without regard to the public interest. The need for control is reinforced by the uncertainty of the economic policy appropriate to a public service; most of the nationalized industries are not, and cannot be, run purely on what are loosely called 'business principles'. Nevertheless, our inquiries leave us in little doubt that the effective and economical long-term planning of investment is disrupted by the sudden and unforeseeable edicts from the Government. We think that this is certainly harmful to morale, and that there is a strong presumption that it is harmful to technical progress.

Changes in the overall financial allocation have to be translated into changes in detailed projects; and delays are then liable to be introduced, because of the great size of the organizations. If there is a large delegation of authority, plans may become inconsistent, and the subordinate bodies may use their powers too freely without adequate consideration. Thus the Advisory Committee on Organization reported to the National Coal Board in 1955 that the authority of Area General Managers to embark on capital expenditure up to £100,000 was excessive, and that larger schemes were not being submitted to the Board in a satisfactory and well-thought-out way. In 1952 and 1953 the delay 'at the top', between receipt of a scheme and its approval, averaged seven to nine weeks. Greater centralization of decision would have to be carefully planned if it were not to produce undue delay. The report of the (Herbert) Committee of Inquiry into the Electricity Supply Industry (Cmd. 9672, 1956) leaves an impression of undue centralization. They trace the history of a typical project originating from a District Manager and say: 'At no stage in its career will this project be consider individually or in detail by any body of people who are responsible for financing it. The responsibility for financing it lies at no point lower than the Central Authority and by the time the project reaches that level it has passed beyond the limits of effective criticism.' The Herbert Committee therefore proposed that Area Boards should go direct to the market for their own capital requirements.

The history of large undertakings in private industry shows clearly that there is no easy answer to this conflict between central control and local responsibility. We mention the matter here because, as seen by the people actually in charge of the execution of projects, the uncertainty produced by the ultimate Government control is increased by the doubts and delays of the working of a complicated machinery.[1]

[1] See *Industry and Technical Progress*, p. 125.

Four   The variety of business motives

We have discussed in the last two chapters the technical opportunities of investment, and the uncertainty which commonly surrounds its outcome. We now draw closer to the actual questions of decision, by two stages. In this chapter we discuss the broad motives influencing business men in their attitude to investment in equipment, and in the next chapter we discuss the influences operative in particular decisions to invest.

Is it true that the chief motive of businesses in a private-enterprise system is to make a profit, and usually to make as big a profit as they can manage? Our theme in this chapter will be that this simple statement of motive conceals a host of difficulties. What does a 'maximum profit' mean? How hard do business men really try to attain it? Are there other motives, subsidiary to or competing with the profit motive, which influence business behaviour? The examination of such questions reveals a great variety of attitudes, and two business men who both say that they invest to increase their profits may be found on a more searching examination to mean quite different things.

First, however, let us consider the implications of the simple statement that firms try to make their money profits as big as possible. This is part of the general assumption of 'rationality'; and it would seem that if a firm acts rationally, a knowledge of the production and market possibilities should enable an economist, without painstaking empirical inquiries, to deduce or predict what the firm will do. The problem is admittedly complicated by the uncertainty of the future, but it should still be possible in principle to deduce what the firm will do in response to particular expectations about the future, whether or not those expectations are destined to be fulfilled.

The prediction about the firm's actions in relation to new investment would be made as follows. Roughly speaking, the firm will buy a new machine when the expected rate of return is better than the rate of return which could be obtained by an alternative use of the resources of the business. The alternative uses include the investing of money outside the firm, and the 'rate of interest' obtained by such investment (e.g. on the Stock Exchange) will bear some relation to the rate at which the firm could borrow. Another way of looking at the matter, therefore, is to say that the firm will buy a new machine if it yields a profit over the cost of borrowing the money to pay for it; or perhaps we should say a 'sufficient' profit, because the accounting return to capital (the revenue *less* the costs, including depreciation) must be big enough to encourage the owners not to pull out of business and spend their capital. The necessary hope of profit on new investment will arise for such reasons as the expansion of demand, the opening up of new markets for attractive new products, and the invention of less costly processes.

It follows from this theory[1] that investment will fall if changes in the supply of savings push up the rate of interest, or if investment opportunities are used up at a greater rate than they are created by invention and by the expansion of the economic system. If, furthermore, we take account of expectations about the uncertain future, investment will fall when through political, digestive, or other changes investors take a more gloomy view of the future state of business.

The first obstacle with which such a theory is faced is the assertion that there may be other grounds for action, as rational as, or more rational than, the making of as much profit as possible.[2] A quiet life, or the enjoyment of public esteem, may appear to the business man more important than the squeezing of the last penny of profits from the stones of circumstance. If finance is easily available, investment may be pushed beyond the point of greatest profit because high investment confers prestige, or the sense of power over a great industrial empire. On the other hand, investment may be held back by a reluctance to experiment or to expand beyond the convenient span of control of existing managers; the attractions of profit may not be enough to persuade the firm to reorganize its management structure. Many family firms (as we found in our inquiries) will not expand their assets to grasp opportunities of profit, because to do so would endanger family control by introducing outside capital.

---

[1] For a more sophisticated discussion, see the Appendix.

[2] See, e.g., Scitovsky, 'A Note on Profit Maximization', *Review of Economic Studies*, 1943, pp. 57–60 Higgins, 'Elements of Indeterminacy', *American Economic Review*, September 1939, pp. 468–79; Hicks, 'The Theory of Monopoly', *Econometrica*, February 1935, pp. 1–20.

The chance that considerations other than the greatest profit will enter in is increased by the separation of ownership and management in the larger companies. Directors and managers can over considerable periods withstand the desire of the shareholders for a better reward, and, if they are thus able to build up large reserves, they are set free to pursue purposes other than the maximization of profits. Another aspect of this separation of ownership and management (with its accompanying possibility of a clash of interests between shareholders, debenture holders, and managers) is that managers who do not own many shares may be more interested in an increase of their own power and financial reward than in the increase of dividends for shareholders. Thus, when faced with a choice between investment in the extension of existing lines of activity and investment in new types of product or process, which might lead to the growth of new divisions of the company, the managers might choose the latter, though its potential profitability might be less.

Some of these speculations about the existence of motives other than the straight maximization of profits are confirmed by observation. Joel Dean[1] argues that top managers who have little to gain from higher profits, but much to lose from corporate re-organization should plans financed with outside capital misfire, are reluctant to borrow or even to raise funds from equity sources; the managers thus recommend the retention of profits, even though the return from their use within the firm may fall below yields available elsewhere. This attitude can certainly be observed in some firms. Brockie and Grey have reported that many firms are not interested in profitable investment in other companies unless they can acquire management control.[2] P. W. S. Andrews and Elizabeth Brunner, after examining investment in the United Steel Company, found that prospective money yields were 'decisive influences only for what are, on the whole, relatively minor expenditures upon replacements on grounds of obsolescence. . . . Most capital expenditure is decided on general policy grounds and is more a matter of the general development of the Company and of the growth of its output than of factors relating narrowly to a particular project's earning power.'[3] In our

[1] *Capital Budgeting*, New York, Columbia University Press, 1951.

[2] *Economic Journal*, December 1956, p. 667.

[3] *Capital Development in Steel*, Blackwell, 1951, p. 356. See also Chester Barnard in *Change and the Entrepreneur*, Harvard University Press, 1949; P. Sargant Florence, *The Logic of British and American Industry*, Routledge, 1953; M. W. Reder, 'Marginal Productivity Theory Reconsidered', *Journal of Political Economy*, October 1947, pp. 450–8.

own studies we have found many firms whose estimates of the profit to be expected from new developments were so vague that it seemed reasonable to conclude that they were not trying to maximize profit. Such a conclusion may, however, be misleading, for some of these firms use other rules (e.g. to follow the actions of competitors, or to maximize prospective turnover) which may lead to the same result as would be attained by an explicit attention to the making of a maximum profit.

As another example, consider the following comment by a correspondent in a large firm in a modern industry, which has embarked on expensive new developments:

Faith has, I am sure, played a large part in our investment. Initially I doubt if any tests of worthwhileness were done, and even as late as 1955 new capital was injected on the scantiest of market appraisals. I realise that this faith could be related to the profit motive, but this would, I think be incorrect. I wonder whether in this firm we are genuinely 'business men'? On the whole, I think not . . . the Research Department has been the recruiting ground for many a manager; I do not believe that they easily change from test tubes to the profit motive.

It is a mistake, however, to be over-enthusiastic in stating the limitations of the idea of profit maximization. In a competitive economy, making as much profit as possible is a condition of survival, and (whatever the ideas of business men about what they *ought* to do) natural selection will weed out those who do not *in fact* pay a due regard to profit. The firm which gave rise to the quotation in the last paragraph survives because it chooses its research projects well, and the faith of its scientists-turned-managers turns out on the average to yield profitable results. But, of course, in some trades there is so little competition, either direct or indirect, that business men can be free to use a rule of behaviour other than the maximization of profits.

If we accept the need to seek profits, how shall these profits be defined? Since the future is uncertain, the *period of time* involved in an investment plan is important. If you put up a new factory in 1960, you do not necessarily expect that it will yield maximum profit, or indeed any profit at all, in 1961. But what is the period to be? A large and successful firm with big reserves and ready access to the capital market is in a much better position to undertake an investment project, of a kind which may become very profitable only after a long period of development, than a newer or smaller firm would be.

Profit maximization, in other words, must be thought of in relation to obstacles which vary from firm to firm and from industry to industry.

The question of the period over which profits might be maximized is, of course, related to the firm's power of survival. We have found several examples in our case-studies of firms which have been forced to concentrate on investment projects showing quick yields, since otherwise they would endanger their capacity to finance a growth in stocks and work in progress. Such firms are typically young and small but just reaching a critical and expensive stage in their growth. We have also found other firms which felt that their long-run profitability would be best served by investment in projects which could not yield a financial return for perhaps ten years. Examples can be found in the aircraft industry, and in many research fields; for instance, the work of certain private firms in relation to atomic energy, or (earlier) the investments in research which produced synthetic indigo and nylon.

Another potential ambiguity arises from a hidden assumption about the kind of world in which the firm operates. When under competitive conditions we say that a firm maximizes profits we imply that it is adjusting its *output or costs* to achieve this, since the *price* is determined by market forces over which it has no control. Under competition, producers invest in new methods to cut costs and create profits; the profits induce others to follow suit, and prices fall accordingly. In monopoly or semi-monopoly conditions, however, firms can do more than just alter their output. They may decide to keep prices up, and to share their monopoly gains with their workers; they may pass on the fruits of technical progress to consumers in the form of lower prices. Under conditions which are not fully competitive, a firm may have freedom to pursue aims other than maximization of profits; but even if it thinks first of profits, its actions will clearly depend on whether it is thinking in terms of falling prices and a growing market, or of high prices and a restricted market.

Yet another possibility of ambiguity and confusion arises from the difference between desired and achieved profit. The fact that a firm is observed not to achieved the highest possible profit is no proof that it does not *desire* it. It may have made its decisions on insufficient information. It may, after committing itself to a particular line of activity, have run across resistance from lower managers or workers who do not wish their habits or interests to be disturbed. The top managers themselves may lack the capacity to judge a changing situation and to adapt their plans to it. Thus even a decision which was reasonable on the information available at the time when it was made may go sadly wrong. One should not confuse the efficiency of *choice* of objectives with efficiency in *pursuing* them.

Again, do firms consciously relate each substantial investment decision to an aim of maximizing profit, or are they satisfied with a good profit record on the average of a series of investments? Both attitudes are found; some firms make careful estimates, and relate them to a rule about expected yield; others back their hunches or the faith of their scientists, in the belief that on the average such a policy will pay off. For reasons such as those mentioned in the last paragraph, the realized profits from individual investments vary greatly, so that (however careful the attention given to each investment before it is made) it will in fact only be possible to assess the adequacy of a profit record on the average of a series of ventures.

Finally, we must distinguish between the maximization of profit as a guide in the choice of investment projects and the desire to make profit as a spur to activity. One is like the rails, guiding a train to its right destination; the other like the engine which pulls it there. The arguments and observations which suggest that, in the real world, the desire to make profit is by no means all-important, apply in many cases to the 'motive power', the general incentive to get on with the job. But even if this is not a matter of profit, it does not follow that investment will be pushed in unprofitable directions. The power of ambition, the desire for status and security, the urge to conformity with the group—all these may be important influences on the activity of business men, but they are like railway engines, prime movers which operate along fixed rails. The form of society and of its institutions may ensure that profit is not forgotten; but the degree to which it remains dominant differs in different sectors of the economy. Thus investment behaviour may be different in the private and the public sectors of economic activity, and it may differ considerably in the public sector between corporations such as the Coal Board and British Railways, which are supposed to cover their costs, and activities such as building roads, bridges, schools, and hospitals. Furthermore, the allocation of capital expenditure between various projects within (say) I.C.I. may be much more closely related to the maximization of profit than is the Government allocation of capital expenditure between the coal industry, British Railways, and the Ministry of Transport road programme. About 25 per cent of fixed investment is made on Government and local-authority account, about 20 per cent by the nationalized industries, and only 55 per cent for private firms and individuals. The differences produced by different attitudes in these sectors cannot, therefore, be ignored.

We thus have plenty of reason to expect a great variety and complexity in the broad motives which influence business men in their reactions to the technical opportunities of investment. But the divergence from the principle of profit maximization is the less likely—

    1 the greater the degree of competition, direct or indirect, and
    2 the greater the importance in the company of a specialist function of creating and evaluating technical and market possibilities.

For the greater the degree of competition, the smaller the margin of profit is likely to be, and the greater the pressure to find really productive projects; and the more stress there is on research and on evaluation, the more information there will be available as the basis for decisions, and the more people there will be with an interest in ensuring that a 'rational' choice is made. We discuss this second point further below (pp. 48–50).

The varied and complex picture is blurred in outline still further by the effect of uncertainty. This may, for instance, cause a firm to feel that it can do no better than use some crude 'rule-of-thumb'— for instance, that an investment project is worthwhile if under present conditions of price and cost it would 'pay for itself' in three or four years. Alternatively, an attempt may be made to 'creep up on a problem' by investing a relatively small sum as a trial—as in the example on page 79. Or a firm may be deliberately cautious, keeping back in liquid form some resources which, on the face of it, it ought to invest, because this extra liquidity makes it possible for things to be changed as circumstances alter for better or for worse.

When conditions of supply and demand are changing, adaptations to past change may not be completed before adaptation to fresh change is required. When we combine the impact of change with that of uncertainty the chance that the firm will be forced to adopt rule-of-thumb methods of behaviour is increased. In view of the number of decisions to be taken and the amount of information required but unprocurable, a firm may decide to watch such things as the liquidity position, the share of the market, and the profit margins, and to take protective action if they fall below 'danger level'.

For the same reason it may base its planning on the attainment of an increased volume of output or an improved share of the market as a rule-of-thumb way of reaching its main objective.

Let us now approach the matter another way, by looking at the different patterns of behaviour of the different types of firm and industry covered by our case-studies—types which are defined, and whose general nature is discussed, in *Industry and Technical Progress*. First of all, it is clear that investment in innovation is not a necessary consequence of competition. Competition may lead to technical progress if it is supported by a supply of scientists and technologists and by an appropriate provision for research and development, and if its stimulating effects are not outweighed by the uncertainty it creates. Without these conditions, however, one may have keen competition but continuing technical backwardness. A technologist in a science-based industry, looking at the work of (say) a craft industry, may consider that what he sees is highly inefficient, and yet the managers in the craft industry may feel certain that they have used all their opportunities to cut costs relative to revenues; and indeed, they may have done all within their capacity. By 'capacity' here is meant not only the capacity to introduce new technical methods but also the capacity to introduce new management structures. In many 'craft' firms we find top managers apparently unwilling to introduce a change of technical process, or a new management structure, which would involve the recruitment of highly paid functional specialists (such as technologists, scientists, or cost accountants), because it would upset the old departmental managers who have spent a long time 'coming up the hard way'. This unwillingness is not due to a sentiment which over-rides the consideration of profit, but to doubt and fear—that if Joe, who knows the craft secret of the process, goes the firm will be helpless, or that if workers resist the innovation the consequent loss would not be outweighed by the advanatges of the new process. Because of this fear and doubt, technical opportunities of investment are wasted.

This attitude is typical of managers in parochial[1] firms in all industries; they may be content with a low level of achievement because they have never overcome, or have never been forced to face, the problems inherent in change. They have no idea that a better

[1] See *Industry and Technical Progress*, p. 108: 'By a parochial firm we mean one which is confined within self-imposed and narrow limits; it is an object of its policy, or a least a result of that policy in practice, that it should not look outside itself for ideas.'

way of doing things is within their reach. An industry slumbering in this state may be jolted into a new outlook by developments abroad or by the competition of substitutes, and it may then begin to recognize its collective interest in research and education and in the use of knowledge developed elsewhere.[1] At this point investment opportunities may be seen or created, and used as part of the fight for survival.

It is possible to reach equilibrium with a relatively low level of technical achievement (and a relatively low level of capital expenditure) in an industry of parochial firms. But even in non-parochial firms the standards of achievement will be related to the conception of the possible. Gundar Haegg ran his fastest mile in 4 minutes 1 second, but it does not follow that he was an inferior runner to Bannister, who cut the time below 4 minutes, or to Ibbotson, who has run a mile in 3 minutes 57 seconds. Ibbotson's success was made possible by Haegg and Bannister; for in the months or years when Ibbotson's speed as a miler was being determined, his training schedules were based on the knowledge that a 4-minute mile was humanly possible, and that to run a mile in under 4 minutes was a condition of winning races. In the same way the speed with which firms introduce profitable new products and processes is in large measure determined by a sense of what is possible. The efficiency of innovational policy will depend, as in athletics, on a combination of pressure and mental outlook.

As a firm becomes more sophisticated in its techniques of direction and management, it takes steps to develop potential investment opportunities, to reduce the number of unknowns in its investment projects, and to keep abreast of scientific and technical developments throughout industry. Under these conditions, subject to an effective full-employment programme on the part of the Government, the distinction between desired and achieved profit becomes less important and (subject to certain later qualifications, e.g. about ways of forecasting) the significance of objectives other than profit is reduced. This is so for two main reasons. First, the discovery of investment opportunities requires research and development, and if research and development are efficiently conducted they will be directed towards the projects most profitable to the firm. A group will have been created within the firm whose power and prestige are tied up with rapid and profitable technical change. Second, a firm consciously

---

[1] For examples of this process in the pottery and building-materials industries, see *The Structure of British Industry*, ed. D. Burn (Cambridge University Press, 1958)

looking for investment opportunities is likely to be seeking methods of rational choice between the opportunities it finds. This choice will naturally tend to be based on figures of savings or surpluses in relation to cost; and therefore it is likely that the greatest yield or profit will be used as a means of making the decision. (The ranking procedure is, as we shall see later, not quite as rational as it looks:cf. p. 74–5.)

A further subdivision used in *Industry and Technical Progress* was between craft, engineering, and 'modern' industries. In this chapter it is useful to divide each of these types into competitive and noncompetitive industries. We can then consider the relevance for each of the idea of maximizing profits, and how far it affects investment behaviour.

1 In a *competive craft industry* firms do their best to maximize their profits, but they do not usually do all the investment which is profitably open to them. Investment takes place largely because of the deterioration of existing equipment and, as costing is likely to be primitive, the incentive to invest will simply be the desire to keep going. We have already discussed the way in which outside pressures may bring about a change of outlook in such an industry.

2 In a *non-competitive craft industry*, under no pressure from substitutes, the owners and managers are free to react (if they wish) to the desire for a quiet and comfortable life, made possible by high profits from limited and protected markets. Sargant Florance suggests[1] that the relatively poor performance of British industry between 1880 and 1930, when compared with that of other industrial countries, was due to the large proportion of its output controlled by heads of family firms who react less keenly to higher profit, and re-invest less of that profit. This may happen in an uncompetitive craft industry, though we doubt whether any relative stagnation of British industry can be explained in such terms.[2]

It is in the nature of craft firms that they are small and that the management structure is simple. In the second class of industry, engineering, there is no such restriction—the firms range from small workshops to large factories engaged in mass production. In this group, therefore, there are firms with very simple and unspecialized

[1] *The Logic of British and American Industry*, Routledge, 1953, p. 320. See also Chapter 14 of Burn, op. cit.
[2] The explanation does not fit the pottery industry: see B. R. Williams in Burn, op. cit.

management structures, and also firms with a highly complex management.

3 In *competitive engineering industry* the probability that investment opportunities will be exploited is somewhat greater than in the craft or traditional industries—provided that firms are open to receive new ideas at all. Some firms we classify as 'adoptive', that is to say ready to use ideas coming to them from outside, and in the engineering industry there is likely to be a good deal of pressure to use ideas coming from customers or suppliers of machinery—and in consequence an incentive to invest. Three-quarters of all the engineering firms we visited did to some extent create technical opportunities for themselves, and they thus have design staff anxious that they should meet competition by innovation.

4 In *non-competitive engineering industry* (e.g. firms who are sole suppliers of some specialized type of plant) it seems to us that a great deal depends on the ability of the firm to attract good people from the limited supply of technologists and skilled managers, and on its ability to adapt its organization to new forms of production. A firm with strong and well-organized design and development departments and lively management is keen to use innovations, if only for reasons of professional pride. A firm which (perhaps because its industry is considered 'old-fashioned') finds it hard to attract lively minds may stick in the mud, content to supply its protected market with its traditional product.

5 In *'modern' industry* whether competitive or non-competitive, a strong pressure to invest in new types of plant or new products is created by the scientific and technical staff, who in this type of industry have a high importance and status. The rate of technical change is usually high, and, as a condition of survival, emphasis must be given to research and development and to the right choice of the investment projects suited to the firm. The 'modern' industries show some of the best examples of attention to forecasting and of thought given to the choice of the right amount and form of capital expenditure. The nature of the industry is in this case more important than the competitiveness of its market.

It can be seen from all this discussion of the variety of reactions and motives operative in different types of firm that a 'general theory' of investment decisions stands little chance of copying with the complexity of the real world.

Five The grounds for deciding to invest

In the last chapter we tried to show the variety of general motives which may influence the investment policy of firms. In this chapter we discuss what it is that causes a firm to make a particular investment.

A simple but common reason for a particular investment is that it has become necessary as a condition for the survival of the firm. Equipment wears out and requires replacement; methods or products become obsolete. As we have seen (p. 15), the mere act of replacement commonly contains an element of innovation. This is especially likely if surrounding circumstances (e.g. the availability of labour) have changed since the original investment. For example, the shortage of skilled labour after the Second World War gave the jute industry an incentive to instal new types of spinning-machine, and the pottery industry an incentive to instal tunnel ovens and semi-automatic making equipment.[1] It was a condition of survival in the post-war world to replace plant and machines, often with plenty of life left in them, by new types which were more economical of labour. Difficulty in getting raw materials has a similar effect: thus, a shortage of coal induced many firms to instal automatic stokers and more economical grates.

Thus in a changing world the desire to survive, implicit in the very nature of a joint-stock company, produces a pressure to invest, and often to invest in innovation. The pressure is made greater by competition, actual or expected. The introduction of a new process which reduces cost, or of a new product which diverts demand from an old product, potentially reduces the profits of others. It thus gives the competitors an incentive to restore their position by bringing in a new process or re-designing an old product or creating a new one— all actions which entail capital expenditure.

The function of competition in forcing business men to instal up-to-date plant and equipment has always been an important one in market economies. Despite quaint but common notions to the contrary, economists have never supposed that business men were so built as to strive unceasingly to find the best products and the least

[1] See *Industry and Technical Progress*, Appendix III.

costly processes. They supposed that competitive pressure was required for this: sellers, competing for custom, force prices and profit margins down, and in competition profit margins can only be restored by improving methods of manufacture or the quality of products.

Once competition exists—direct competition between producers making the same commodity and indirect competition between producers catering for the same need—the desire to be prepared to meet it may indirectly bring about investment in new plant and equipment. Much of the work of research and development departments is concerned with getting or keeping ahead of both direct and indirect competition.

This competitive pressure to make innovations may reach back to suppliers. Thus a multiple store (such as Marks and Spencer) sometimes reaches back to suppliers and presses them to instal new plant and machinery to produce goods of lower cost or higher quality. A similar influence has been exercised by the electrical industry on the makers of electrical porcelain in the pottery industry, and by the steel industry on the makers of refractory bricks.

These pressures are closely related to the desire to survive, and clearly to survive is a condition of making profit. Profit opportunities, given by the expansion of demand or the creation of new processes or of new products, provide further incentives to invest. The creation of new products and new processes is increasingly the outcome of research and development; and once a firm makes arrangements for research and development it builds up from within a pressure to invest in new products and processes, for this will be the function and the interest of the technologists and scientists so employed. In a competitive situation it becomes difficult to distinguish the pressures to invest which come from the impulse to survive, from the financial incentive to use a profit opportunity, and from the interested push from development departments (or, for that matter, from sales staff).

We have re-examined 204 cases involving significant innovation, provided by 116 firms in our original case-studies. The types of innovation involved were as follows:

	Cases
Product new or differing from the normal range	105
Product improved	13
Process new, to give increased integration of processes . . .	16
Process new or improved, to make possible considerable expansion in production	8
Other changes in methods of production	62
	204

In considering the classifications which follow, it must be remembered that our material (being based on identifiable and significant innovations) under-represents the host of small improvements in products and processes, brought about (for instance) by improvements in materials or in the machines offered by the trades' suppliers.

Just over half of the innovations were ascribed by the firms concerned to definite causes, such as the pressure of competition or of excess demand. For those so ascribed, the alleged causes were distributed as follows:

	Percentage of innovations
Desire to overcome labour shortage	5
,, ,, materials shortage	12
Desire to meet excess demand	10
Demands by customers for new types or qualities of product .	12
Desire to use the work of research and development departments	18
Direct pressure of competition (i.e. copying or fore-stalling rival firms)	10
Force of example of firms (etc.) other than immediate rivals (i.e. successful trials of product or process in other industries or in other countries)	33
	100

These imputed origins are, however, an unsatisfactory basis of classification, because there is room for differences of interpretation as to what induced the innovation—and it may have been induced by several co-operating causes. For example, some of the innovation ascribed to research and development and to successful trials in other countries or industries were in fact sought out and developed or adopted because of the desire to strengthen the competitive position of the firm. We have therefore classified the innovations as *passive* and *active*. In making a *passive* innovation the firm is responding to direct market pressure, as shown by excess demand or by developing competition and falling profit margins. These are the innovations of which business men say, 'Obviously we just *had* to do it.' In making an *active* innovation the firm is deliberately searching for new markets and techniques, even though there may be no direct market pressure to do so.

The 116 firms who gave us information about clear and significant cases of innovation may be classified in the following way:

Number of innovations	Number of firms	Innovations	
		Active	Passive
1	65	25	40
2	25	30	20
3	16	38	10
4 (or more)	10	27	14
	116	120	84

It will be seen from this table that 40 of the firms that made only one innovation made only passive innovations. Five other firms, with more than one innovation, made only passive innovations and provided another 12 cases. The majority of firms in this sample made both active and passive innovations. The 26 firms with three or more innovations provided 55 per cent of the cases of active innovation and 30 per cent of the cases of passive innovation. While the overall percentage was 60 per cent active[1] and 40 per cent passive, for the firms with three or more innovations the percentages were 72 and 28.

Where a firm considers investment outlays under the impetus of a direct pressure to survive, there may be no strong incentive to calculate the yield on capital expenditure. The issue often seems very simple, namely, that 'to compete we need a modern piece of equipment that firms a and b have sold to our competitors y and z', or 'our machines are now so expensive to maintain and cause so much hold-up or spoiled work that we can't afford to keep them'. The explicit calculation of yield is, in such circumstances, likely only where doubts arise as to the wisdom of reinvesting capital in the industry at all, or where, to use new techniques, the firm has to be reorganized on a larger scale or in a different pattern, or where new capital has to be raised. This is why it is rare in technically stagnant industries (whose decisions are mainly passive) to find much attention given to detailed calculations of yield, for this would involve the careful costing of operations as well as consideration of production and sales plans (or prospects) for future years. For firms that lack the special skills required for this sort of work the number of unknowns will seem too great to make the effort appear sensible.[2]

Where the pressure to invest is less direct, the sense of an opportunity to make profits from capital expenditure becomes more important. How do firms react to this prospect? How high does pros-

[1] But see page 71.
[2] Cf. *Industry and Technical Progress*, pp. 178–83.

pective yield need to be to induce the capital expenditure? How is the prospective yield calculated?

In the sample of 116 firms, 18 firms claimed to set a definite percentage prospective yield on investment in innovation below which they would not invest. In most cases this was expressed in terms of the number of years in which a project would pay for itself, and to avoid ambiguity the calculations of all the firms have been expressed in that way.

Pay-off period in years	Number of companies
2	1
3	3
4	5
5	2
6	2
10	5

In the firms with pay-off periods of less than ten years it was agreed that there were particular cases of new-product and (particularly) new-process developments where (due to 'the national interest', the pressure of competition, or the absence of risk) a lower yield would be acceptable.

We can now supplement the earlier studies by using various extra bits of information about expected yield which have reached us from a number of firms and nationalized undertakings. We must warn the reader, however, that (as we show later, p. 74–5) the concept of 'yield', like damask, can look different according to the angle from which it is viewed. Some firms set their expectations low, but load their estimates with allowances for contingencies; other firms make bold and optimistic estimates, but set them against a high standard of yield. The following extracts from letters and reports reveal some of this complexity, as well as the different ideas of yield in different firms:

(a) 'New investment has to earn 15% on total capital employed, and new schemes for marginal increments of capital are certainly assessed on this criterion. . . . I suppose that any "animal spirits" which may be around are subsumed in our estimates of demand. For instance, one factor may be the rate of expansion of air travel; we shall certainly put this at something higher than 10% per annum—which must mean that we are assuming the continuation of fairly buoyant conditions. Why earn 15%? I don't know the answer, except that if you plan for 15 you might get 10. . . .' (Metal manufacturing, investment involving 'active' innovation.)

(b) 'The return on capital (shown as varying between an expected 4%

and an expected 34%) is the percentage of the profit, after charging full operating cost and depreciation, to the capital investment, fixed assets being included at cost. No adjustment is made for research and development expenditure . . . nor is allowance made for interest on capital during the construction period. . . . Some projects comprise the first plants on a new factory site, with consequential high capital costs and heavy administrative and other overhead costs. On the other hand, later projects can utilise spare capacity installed in the first instance and so show a very substantial return on capital. . . .' (Large firm with varied types of investment.)

(c) 'We expect 20% gross yield overall on big schemes—more on a small job—though we do not make these expectations public. We ignore the possibility of a recession, assuming this to be allowed for in the 20%. We make our calculations on the basis of present prices and costs, assuming that in future the price of our product will rise at least as fast as costs. . . .' (Large firm in heavy industry.)

(d) 'The considerations are the length of sales life of the product, the market position, the relation to the company's existing activities, the availability of factory space and money—and only then the earning capacity. Products require as much working capital as fixed capital; and on the two together we expect at least 10%, usually 15 or 20%, but 30% on difficult or risky projects. For risky projects there is also a tendency to charge a high rate of depreciation before calculating the return.' (Chemical firm.)

(e) 'We assume that new equipment will work at 80% of capacity, but we also make estimates at 100%, 70% and 50% of capacity. Production costs are taken as the present costs of raw materials and services unless we know that cost is going to move abnormally. . . . The cost of capital equipment is assumed to be the currect cost plus provision for inflation. . . . We might put in a plant with a low yield if otherwise we would lose a market for a standard product. . . . The usual expected yield is 20%, before tax and before paying interest on capital.' (Chemical firm.)

(f) 'The yield expected is normally 20% though some lower yields are accepted on monopoly products, for which we have policy of a low prices. There is a tendency to throw good money after bad; it is difficult to cut off uneconomic projects and failures early enough.' (Large firm in modern industry.)

(g) 'The yield expected is relatively low, 10–12% after allowing for replacement cost depreciation. Current prices and conditions are assumed in making estimates.' (Large plants in heavy industry.)

(h) 'We expect at least 20% gross, but sometimes we undertake a project to save (e.g.) skilled labour, and we then might do it even if it showed no saving in cost. Thus after the war we bought machinery without making any calculations in the case of equipment which is non-specific, i.e. for general use in the factory and not assignable to a particular type of output.' (Firm in traditional industry.)

(i) 'If a machine does not pay for itself in five years we would think it a poor buy. It should have been worked hard enough to need replacing in ten years, though in many cases more modern machinery is installed shortly after five years.' (Firm in food industry.)

(*j*) 'The breakdown of our "routine" capital expenditure (i.e. excluding big new projects) is roughly as follows:

Unavoidable expenditure on replacement of plant . . .	7%
Other unavoidable expenditure, including that required for im-proved quality	28%
Projects with an expected yield exceeding 15% . . .	55%
Other expenditure	10%

(Large firm in modern industry.)

Three of the above extracts, duly concealed by anonymity, give partly inconsistent views of the policy of the same firm, as seen by people at different management levels. It must not be supposed, therefore, that the operation of investment policy is tidy and consistent, even in firms which make explicit forecasts.

For comparison, one may take these United States data for 1947 and 1948, which related to machine tools. The difference between the two columns is apparently due to differences in the form of question asked.[1]

Pay-off period in years	1947 survey (560 companies)	1948 survey (51 companies)
1	4	14
2	13	41
3	23	19
4	22	8
5	24	8
Over 5	14	10

A survey in Minneapolis in 1950 showed pay-off periods clustered around 1 to 3 years for minor projects and 5 to 7 years for major projects.[2] Other surveys, before the War and since, have suggested that a three-year pay-off period is common; but such data are difficult to interpret without knowing what is included in the estimates in each case.

Comparisons between firms and between countries on the basis of such figures should in fact be treated with considerable caution. Apart from the problem of 'written-in' gloom or optimism, the whole basis of estimates can differ between firms or industries and between

[1] Quoted in G. Terborgh, *Dynamic Equipment Policy*, McGraw Hill, 1949.
[2] W. W. Heller, 'The Anatomy of Business Decisions', *Harvard Business Review*, March 1951, p. 101.

countries in two important respects—the allowance for taxation and the definition of the capital to which the yield relates. Some firms calculate yield after allowing for expected tax liabilities, others make no such allowance. Some firms calculate the yield on the value of the fixed investment only, while others calculate it on fixed investment *plus* the addition expected to be required to working capital. Sometimes there are year-to-year variations in the practice of a single firm.

The firms which do not have a definite minimum pay-off period may be arranged in two broad groups. The first includes 34 firms which made estimates of prospective costs and revenues, but which thought either that there was no *one* pay-off period above which investment was not justified, or that they could not rely on yield estimates sufficiently to use them as a deciding factor. Indeed some of these firms argued that the element of 'commercial acumen' cannot be reduced to rules or described in objective terms. But in some cases the commercial acumen is exercised on a list of projects which have already been through a prospective-yield sieve in the development departments, so that the claim of the final decision-takers to a kind of second sight is not important.

We also include in the first group those firms which base their judgement on the estimated cost of the innovation and the turnover which might arise from it. This can be regarded as equivalent to a rough-and-ready 'prospective yield' criterion. It means that the prospective market is thought to be big enough for the firm to include in the price a sum sufficient to enable it to write off the equipment in an appropriate number of years.

In the second group were 64 firms which proceed to investment decisions without making a yield calculation, either implicit or explicit. In this group are firms which judge that they must use 'modern methods' to survive, firms which take up a new product or process simply because it has been successful in another industry or another country, firms which introduce new processes that appear likely to show a 'big saving', and firms which find it possible to 'creep up on a problem' by trying out a new product or process in a small way.

This second group includes firms which are reacting defensively to forces which endanger their existence. Thus it includes 30 of the 45 firms which made only passive innovations. But it also includes firms which are aggressively seeking profit outlets, and which do not quantify their forecasts for a number of reasons. In some firms the decision-taking process is personal and the decision based on mental sums or 'back-of-the-envelope' estimates. In other firms (and this is quite a reasonable procedure where change is neither rapid nor extensive) one or two critical factors, such as quality or price, are considered in relation to other factors that are implicitly assumed to be unchanged. In still other cases, where change is rapid, extensive reliance on guesswork figures may be foolish because of the absence of costing, budgeting, and market research. There the firm may 'back a hunch' or rely on a number of favourable pointers to success.

From the nature of our information it is not possible to say much about inter-industry variations in the required prospective yield. There are, however, a number of fairly obvious general tendencies. The first is that firms in the industries which at the time of our studies were technically most progressive stated the *highest* prospective yields as a precondition of investment in plant and equipment. The second, related to the first, is that firms which expect new plant and equipment to 'pay for itself' in a very short period take a long view about investment in research and development facilities. Third, that industries in which obsolescence is apparently highest seem the least worried by uncertainty about the future.

The explanation of these tendencies as we have derived them from our case-studies is fairly simple. Firms in the technically progressive industries have many projects to choose from. We showed in *Industry and Technical Progress* that the limit to investment in new products and processes is, in such industries, set by the shortage of scientists and engineers or by the difficulty of adapting the organization to higher rates of change. Where there is a high rate of technical change, due to the opportunity for productive industrial research and the employment of large numbers of scientists and technologists in it, firms will expect rapid technical obsolescence or a prompt competitive response which will squeeze profit margins on the new products or processes. Such firms will adopt a different attitude to investment in innovation, because of the nature of research and development. Projects are chosen for development from those research problems which have been solved, and are chosen for investment from those development problems which have been solved. In the process many projects fall by the wayside, though they may be adopted later because of subsequent scientific or technological or market developments; those that remain have already been sifted and weighed within the firm. The research and development departments not only turn out investment projects, and by conducting trials (and maybe market research) reduce the uncertainty attaching to them, but also increase the background knowledge of materials and processes, and provide a 'reserve capacity' to solve unexpected problems thrown up by actions of competitors, suppliers or customers. As for the apparent sense of certainty in the face of uncertain future market conditions, this is to be explained by the high allowance for uncertainty provided by the use of short periods of pay-off for new equipment, and also by the function of research and development in reducing the sense of uncertainty about the costs of operating a new process or the market reaction to a new product.

We have shown that the impulse to make particular investments comes from a variety of sources. The place of individuals in all this is often stressed—after all, we require individuals to decide and to act; and there are occasions when particular individuals dominate even a large organization. In general, however, we need to consider the individual not in isolation, but in relation to the organization. We have mentioned the importance of 'pressure from within the firm' in taking investment decisions. The most important example of this is provided by the role of research and development departments in creating new technical opportunities for investment.

We have given in *Industry and Technical Progress* (Chapters 6 and 12) an account of the way in which research and development is conducted in efficient companies, and an explanation of the different practices of firms relating to the existence and scale of research and development activity. It must be remembered that, judging from our sample, research and development is a well-used management technique in very few firms.

In a greater or lesser degree, those engaged in industrial research and development gather relevant scientific and technical information and relate and apply it to the producing activities of the firm. Where the research and development staff are not simply engaged in technical testing or trouble-shooting, they will be concerned with getting and appraising ideas for different products or processes. Given a reasonably efficient department, the greater the range of considered possibilities, the greater will be the number of potential investment projects. The greater therefore will be the pressure to invest—first, because a large number of investment opportunities will be there ready for use: second, because members of the research and development department will be on the spot with an interest in getting their work turned to good advantage: and third, because it is discouraging to see unused research results pile up, and the firm will risk the loss of good research and development staff if their work is not used.

The greater the range of considered possibilities in relation to financial resources, the greater will be the pressure to rank in order the various ideas for product or process development. The obvious way to rank them when a decision is to be taken by a financier, or by a group consisting of production, sales, and finance staff is in terms of money—and in particular in terms of a forecast relation between earned revenues and incurred costs. This pressure to rank projects in terms of profitability is also exerted at an earlier stage of proceedings. For when there are many development possibilities to consider, some way must be found, in a sensible organization, for deciding which few should use the scarce development resources.

As companies grow in size, management functions become specialized. As companies move from a craft to a modern basis the same thing happens, but in particular, there is a growth in the specialist functions of investigation and evaluation, relative to execution.[1] The attention to investigation (laboratory and market research) and evaluation (technical development work, ranking of projects, operations research, and work study) is marked in science-based firms. The relevant functionaries are often concentrated in special departments —e.g. research and development—but similar functions have to be performed from time to time within production departments. Sometimes specialist help is called in, though for many small things the production department has staff qualified to conduct its own investigation and evaluation. But whatever the degree of specialization the growth of these specialist functions has brought with it a great growth of committees within the firm's management structure, and with it the growth of impersonal decision-taking. With the growth of this form of decision-taking the need to quantify is increased.

This does not mean that the board of directors will always accept the ranking given in papers prepared for it, or will always prefer a project ranked highest in estimated profitability. The directors may not accept the forecasts about future market trends, though this will only affect the ranking for those projects particularly sensitive to an increase or decrease of activity; or they may not accept the forecasts about the market potential of a new product, perhaps because of a better (or worse) knowledge of what competitors are up to; or they

[1] See B. R. Williams, 'Science and Industrial Innovation', *Advancement of Science* December 1956, This growth is being further investigation in a project financed by D.S.I.R.

may, on policy grounds, decide not to enter this or that form of activity implied by a high-ranking project, but decide instead to choose a lower-ranking project which entails a broadening of the basis of operations or a higher degree of integration or a link or joint enterprise with another firm. Nevertheless, there remains the tendency as research and development activity grows to rank projects in monetary terms, and therefore a tendency to choose on this basis, and to find resources for profitable-looking projects. This is why in efficient organizations the incentives to invest given by profit opportunity and by the internal pressures for action merge one into the other.

Six On not investing

There are two reasons for including a chapter 'on not investing' in this book. One is that there is no clear line dividing worthwhile from useless investment projects, and a study of those projects which have been considered, but have failed to gain acceptance, may throw light on the decision process. The other reason is that there are projects, later shown to be or thought to be worthwhile, which originally were not carefully considered. The potentialities of new scientific knowledge, or of an invention, are frequently obscure. If the gap between the new knowledge and its use in innovation is to be bridged there must be an effective system of communication between scientists and inventors, and between them and business men. An efficient system of industrial research and development may also be needed to make the discovery ready for industrial use. There may therefore be a waste of potential innovations because of a missing or ineffective link in the chain of communication, or because there is insufficient attention to industrial research and development. It is because these unconsidered projects may be as significant as the ill-considered and the rejected projects that this chapter is headed 'on not investing' and not 'decisions not to invest'.

We have four broad questions to consider:

1 Does the rule for determining which investments to undertake operate in a reasonable manner?

2 Is the ranking of possible investment projects reasonable, or does some undesirable bias enter in through the method used to calculate or judge the prospects?

3 Do outside causes, such as the difficulty of raising capital, enter in to frustrate projects which the firm concerned is ready to carry out?

4 Do the unconsidered projects occur at random and, whether they do or not, is the likely ratio of considered to unconsidered projects reasonable?

People's views about these broad issues can be seen in some of the jeremiads about the alleged backwardness of British industry in applying science. British industry lags in the application of science, so we are told, because the 'financial heads' of industry are too timid; and this could be taken to mean that these financial rulers set needlessly high standards of prospective yield. It could also mean that unwillingness to venture or to take risks distorts the ranking of investment projects, and excludes some of the most exciting projects made possible by the advance of science.

Unwillingness to venture might be due, however, not to the native or induced caution of the financier, but to a shortage of venture capital; or it might be due to the process of selecting business leaders, as is implied by the assertion that there are 'too few scientists (or too many accountants) in the Boardroom'. If there are too few scientists in the boardroom, there might be in consequence distortion in the ranking of investment projects because of the inability of the directors to judge or appreciate projects which are based on sound scientific principles, even though they are not yet fully proved in practice. Or the ratio of unconsidered to considered projects might be needlessly high because of a failure either to arrange for research and development or to draw on the research and development of others.[1]

We begin by considering those cases in which the rule of decision is provided, explicitly or implicitly, by requiring projects to show a reasonable yield. The standard of reasonableness may be set by comparison with practice in a country considered to be efficient in applying science to industry, or by some judgement about the optimum rate of economic progress. But the 'optimum rate' is a vague and unsatisfactory concept; the best we can do is to see if international comparisons suggest that Britain is setting too high a yield, and is thus excluding worthwhile projects.

Such inquiries as we have been able to make do not support the view that British firms set a higher standard of yield than corresponding firms in other countries; though we have mentioned on p. 45-6 the difficulty of making meaningful comparisons. The evidence of the last chapter suggests that many American firms expect yields much higher than those for the British firms which we mention. This is consistent with our observation that in Britain firms with a high rate of innovation set high prospective yields as a condition for investment. The standard of prospective yield in traditional and stagnant industries is a low one; a low rate of investment must in such cases be

---

[1] *Industry and Technical Progress*, Chapters 12 and 16.

ascribed not to an unreasonable rule for making investment decisions but to the slight attention given by firms to the creation of invest- ment opportunities, and to their cautious attitude to new methods.

Evidence drawn from prospective yields is, of course, inconclusive. Most firms do not make careful calculations of prospective yield, and it is possible that the firms which prefer hunches and vague impres- sions to calculation do not invest in innovation except in conditions where calculation would in fact show high prospects of yield. But we do not find this common. If it were common, it would be inconsistent with our observation about low yields in traditional industries, since these are the industries in which 'quantification' of decisions is least common.

Some firms were concerned in their investment decision with the adoption of techniques already proved elsewhere. They could thus make a lower allowance for uncertainty, and often they were also assuming that the method, once proved and adopted, would remain in use for a long time. More generally, where we could translate the thinking or guessing of the firm to an explicit yield basis, the accept- able yield was low; we found only a few exceptions to this among un- progressive firms.

We must also take into account the written-in gloom or optimism of the estimates. It is possible that the paper calculations of a firm indicate that it requires a prospective yield of 10 per cent before it will agree to invest, but that in fact it requires a considerably higher yield. This would happen if the firm is persistently conservative in estimating market prospects or operating costs. The significance of this may be judged from the following two quotations, which are extracts from letters explaining differences between prospective and actual yields. Both firms make explicit estimates of prospective yield.

For some years most of our projects have been successful and the actual yield has far exceeded estimates. This is probably due to the difficulty of estimating markets for new products in our industry, and also because in proposing capital expenditure we tend to be conservative in estimating profit ratios and yields.

Because of human nature, which in business had better be optimistic than pessimistic, there is a tendency for capital expenditure to be under-estimated and yields to be over-estimated. To the extent that estimates cannot be made accurately and have to depend on judgement, the relationship be- tween estimate and 'actual' will reflect the quality of that judgement, and that in turn will reflect the quality and temperature of the man himself.'

Some firms lean to pessimism, others to optimism; we have no sufficient evidence to support a generalization that there is a bias one way or the other. Evidence on this matter is hard to come by, for in most firms the details of the forecasts, or the cost and revenue records for actual operations, or both, are inadequate to support a comparison of actual and expected yields. The facts given in the next chapter (p. 65) suggest that there is no persistent tendency to over-caution. There may, of course, have been a tendency to be over-cautious in estimates during the inter-war period.

Our conclusion so far is that, where the rule of decision is provided, explicitly or implicitly, by a yield requirement, there is no evidence that unreasonably high yields are required, or that estimates are made with undue caution; and that, on the whole, the same conclusions stands for firms which make their decisions on 'hunches' or other grounds difficult to relate to yield. One special case remains for consideration. Some firms make their investment decisions within the framework of a 'master decision' governing the total amount to be spent. Thus some companies have capital budgets, running for a period of years but frequently revised, based on the spending of the surplus after a rate of dividend considered appropriate for the trade. Some firms have a 'master decision' to produce two or three new products each year; some have a definite idea of the rate of change which they can effectively manage; some fix their investment expenditure in relation to estimates or target figures for turnover. Clearly the wooden application of a 'master decision' in circumstances in which it had ceased to be appropriate might result in the exclusion of desirable investment, or the inclusion of projects, chosen to fill out the investment budget, which in fact are not worthwhile.

This is a possible danger, but we have no evidence that it is a real one. Firms making such 'master decisions' are often highly progressive, and have given a good deal of attention to the right size of research, development, and innovation. The capital budget, or other overall limitation, is a convenient device for securing clarity of thinking about what the firm could achieve; but if it were found to be obstructing some really worthwhile project, efforts would be made to alter the limits on action. Any obstruction to innovation is set, not by the method of decision, but by the real factors which lie behind it—such as the shortage of capital or of managerial skill.

The next major question is the effectiveness of the ranking or ordering of investment projects, so that the best may be chosen. This setting of the possibilities in order is no easy process; simply to attach to a project an estimate of the prospective percentage annual yield obscures the major difficulties. There is, in the first place, the factor of uncertainty discussed in Chapter III. For the various new processes which a company might develop, there will be differing risks that actual operating costs will diverge considerably from predicted costs. The more the innovation departs from existing practice, or the less that is known of the background scientific principles, the greater the uncertainty. There is no definite scale by which estimates can be adjusted for this uncertainty; in the end, the real question is whether the firm concerned is prepared to venture or not. Where there is in the project something quite new and not yet fully proved, the decisive consideration will be the firm's confidence in its technical assessment. We have found a clear distinction in this respect between firms that have research (or design) and development departments and firms that lack them. The former are more prepared to venture; the reason is partly that confidence is gained from research and development results, and partly that where a firm employs scientists and technologists it is more likely to take the view that, because a new process is based on sound principles, then any teething problems can be overcome. Because the firm possesses technical and scientific staff, it will have a basic confidence in the innovation which the firm without such staff will lack.

This confidence in ability to manage the unforeseen difficulties is less important where the innovation is a new *product* (rather than a *process*) and the buyer is the final consumer. Willingness to calculate the probable yield on investment without 'playing very safe' with the sales estimate then appears to depend on the existence of market surveys, or on the ability to start in a small way and 'creep up on the problem',[1] or on the smallness of the investment in relation to total resources. Without one of these things venturesome projects may be given a ranking that will appear from later knowledge to be unduly low.

There may be other problems other than the unforeseen technical difficulties. If the innovation would require the creation of a new organization—whether a new division within the firm or the setting up of a subsidiary company—the general problem of management becomes important. Unless a firm is confident that it has available, or can obtain by buying another company a suitable and efficient management team, it may rank the project low, even though both

[1] See p. 79.

technical and market assessment point to the possibility of successful innovation. This was expressed forcefully by the Technical Director of one large firm: 'At the risk of emphasizing the obvious I must express the firmest conviction that the biggest single factor industry has to take into account is the suitability and efficiency of the Management team available at the right time for deployment in the execution of the innovation.' Another person, in a similar position, comments: 'It is no use erecting a large new factory if there is no prospect of running it efficiently or if there are insufficient sales staff of the required calibre to enable the product to be disposed of. This business of the inadequacy of senior high level staff is always the nightmare of any Board of Directors. This applies particularly when proposals for diversification into entirely new lines of business are under consideration.'

We need to take into account here two factors—the amount of innovation that any one firm can undertake during any one period of time, and the supply of people capable of managing an innovation, particularly when that innovation requires the creation of a new organization. A decision to give a low ranking to a project is not necessarily a sign of bias in ranking, though it may well appear so to the scientists involved. A judgement that the project would be too risky because there is not a suitable management team available may be correct. But one must then ask two further questions— whether new management arrangements could increase a firm's capacity to manage change at any one point of time, and whether a greater supply of capable managers could be produced by better training facilities.

It follows that in seeking an answer to the second question— namely, whether there is a bias in the ranking of investment projects that leads to an exclusion of some of the most promising industrial applications of science—it is wise to consider such things as the proportion of firms that employ scientists and technologists, the efficiency of arrangements to test the market reaction to innovation, the financial size of firms in relation to the cost of the potential innovation, and the provision for management training, selection, and research.

Let us look at these issues in turn. American data[1] show a high concentration of research and development facilities in a few, generally large, companies. There is no reason to suppose that the position in Britain is any different, and research and development are indeed

[1] Quoted in *Industry and Technical Progress*, p. 50.

less developed in *private* industry in Britain than they are in America. It is known that in Britain there are very large differences between industries in research expenditure per firm, per employee, or per £ of net output; these are differences between averages for industries, and the differences between firms must be still more extreme. There is therefore every reason to expect that 'efficiency of ranking projects' will vary greatly from industry to industry, and from one firm to another, simply because of the differing degrees of help with technical assessment which are available. It is worth noting that firms with developed research facilities, or with good access to research results, are likely to have a larger flow of innovations coming forward for consideration. The existence of research and development facilities affects both the size of the flow, and the efficiency of using it, and the former effect is probably the most important.

Arrangements for testing market reactions to potential new products must necessarily vary with the nature of the products and their markets. All 'market research' relating to products not yet on the market (and in some cases not yet off the drawing-board) is speculative; but it is at least an attempt to get information on which to base a decision, so that the firm may choose its path in moonlight rather than in complete darkness, and in favourable cases it may lead to a confident prediction of success where otherwise there would have been grave doubts. In our case-studies we found relatively few firms with efficient arrangements for market research; the lack was particularly obvious where the survey of markets and technical salesmanship merge. This arises with products, such as machines, sold to other firms and affecting production methods in those firms: the market cannot be fully tested without giving a technical description of the product and a technical discussion of what it would mean to the buying firm. If an innovation is worthwhile, an estimate of sales based on a technical approach of this kind is likely to show a better prospect than one based on a non-technical inquiry. Insufficient attention to technical salesmanship may thus lead to poor ranking of investment projects.

We are not here thinking of justified fears—where the ranking of a project is low because the project is genuinely poor or uncertain. In some cases the application of the usual tests of economic efficiency indicate that a new product, alleged to be likely to prove unpopular or insufficiently popular, *should* in fact find a large market. In other words, the product can be shown to have, at a given price, properties superior to those of other products on the market; or it is able (when used by another firm) to yield cost savings which would make it 'pay for itself' in a short period. Its failure to find a large market is due both to gaps in the chain of communication of technical information and to the existence of unprogressive and parochial firms. Businesses are customers of other firms, suppliers of other firms, and competitors (or potential competitors) of other firms. What any business can do in the field of innovation depends in considerable measure on what sort of help, stimulus, or pressure it gets from its customers, suppliers, and competitors. We have analysed the importance of this chain of relationships in Chapter 10 of *Industry and Technical Progress*. The relevant point here is that efficient firms may be forced to give a low ranking to promising projects because of defective ranking arrangements in *other* firms, or because of overall inefficiency in other firms. Relations with other firms may also affect the time for which a firm waits for a return on its investment—a matter which we consider further below.

The next possible reason why investment projects may be ranked in a wrong or biased way is that the chance to innovate may come to a firm whose financial strength is not appropriate to the size of the innovation. Thus a discovery made within the firm, which might be highly desirable, and readily capable of successful development within a larger company, is put on one side as being "too big for us to tackle'. (The converse case is when a discovery is ignored because it is too small.) Such things are clearly likely to happen by chance; and we can confirm that cases of apparent low ranking due to these causes can be identified. The loss to the community can, of course, be made good if the firms which find projects too large or too small sell their knowledge on licence to other firms, or enter into joint arrangements to exploit the discovery.

The final cause of bias arises from the inadequacy of the provision for management training, selection, and research. In Britain this provision has been increased since the War, but it is still not very extensive. We have not made a detailed study of the impact of this factor on innovation, but its significance for the problem of 'failure to invest in innovation' may be judged from the high proportion of firms in our case-studies in which the limits to innovation have been set, not by finance, but by problems of management, or the short supply of scientists and technologists, or the inability to get suitable co-operation from other firms.

There is another significant point about the ranking of investment projects—namely, the question of how long a firm may be prepared, or can afford, to wait for the return of a yield on its investment. Some innovations may give a prospect of good and quick returns, others of very good returns after a slow build-up. It might seem possible to deal with this problem by converting the prospective profits on investment in years 1 to n into a 'present value'. This textbook device is valid only if a firm can borrow freely at given market rates, and only if it can afford to be indifferent about the time for which a good management team may be held up in pioneer work. In very many cases neither of these conditions will be applicable. Many firms cannot borrow freely at market rates, and the amount that a firm can borrow, or would be wise to borrow, depends in some measure on the ratio of its risky to its safe undertakings. That being so, a firm may be wise not to undertake an innovation that seems likely to pay well after three or four years, because it would stand in the way of projects which would pay off quicker and could be launched successively, the return on each assisting its successor. This unwillingness to wait is particularly likely (and we find it to be common) where a firm has a shortage of capable development staff —whether on the production or the sales side; for knowing that unforeseen problems, which will need the attention of this staff, may arise, it will not wish its key staff to be over-committed on plans that it could not afford to change. In such a situation the best working rule may be to consider only the prospective surpluses on investment in the first three or four years, and the whole business of 'discounting' them to obtain a present value will be of no great importance.

How can we judge whether a ranking produced from such a nearsighted look into the future has, on balance, a favourable or an unfavourable effect on investment in innovation? There are no clearcut grounds on which this judgement can be made. We can only list the factors that should be taken into account in making the judgement. It is appropriate to take the short view when research and development in the firm is not long established, when there is no considerable fund of knowledge about technological possibilities and their relation to market potential, or when the sums available for investment are small, or the project concerned is large in relation both to investible funds and to the key staff needed to carry it through to success.[1]

It may be appropriate to take a long view when the project is small in relation to the resources of the firm, when success is either a precondition of, or likely to facilitate, the successful application of

[1] *Industry and Technical Progress*, p. 84.

the firm's research and development to a number of other projects, or when the key staff concerned are convinced that the project is very good, that the firm should do it, and that it commands the ability to overcome the obstacles.

We have examined firms where, on the criteria we have just mentioned, excessively short views have been taken, and other firms which have taken excessively long views. It is only possible to give rather impressionistic views on this, but our view after analysis of the case-studies is that if in the period concerned research and development departments had given a greater attention to a programming of research most suited to the financial and market position and the technical capacity of the firms concerned, the time for which firms would have been willing to wait for a return would have been *reduced* rather than increased. With the growth of experience and capacity in research and development departments, and the growth in associated technical manpower, we would expect the time margin to increase. It is perhaps significant that in cases we have examined where Britain lagged in the application of science to industry, or has been alleged so to do, the explanation was not to be found in the taking of too short a view over investment in innovation.[1]

The third broad question for consideration is whether causes outside the firm such as a difficulty of raising capital, enter in to frustrate projects which a firm is ready and willing to carry out. At one stage such frustrations might have included direct Government controls, and inability to find essential materials or essential workers at any price or wage-rate; but these seem to us now of lesser importance, and we shall therefore concentrate attention on financial frustration.

The frustration of progressive firms because of the difficulty of retaining or raising money for development is a matter often misunderstood and sometimes exaggerated. The channels through which finance can flow are numerous and adaptable, and we do not think that there is evidence to support an assertion that there is or has been a general or universal shortage of risk capital. A firm which appears to be frustrated in its innovation by lack of finance may in fact have reached a stage in its development at which any new finance would involve loss of independence or of family control; the

---

[1] See *Industry and Technical Progress*, Chapter 3, which examines a number of cases of alleged British failure to apply science to industry, and suggests explanations such as backwardness in specialized fields of pure science, and failures by industry to reach out and pull in scientific knowledge as fully as it might.

true cause of its frustration may be its unwillingness to face such unwelcome accompaniments of growth.

Nevertheless, during the period of our original case-studies (1954–6) we found evidence of a minority of firms (about 14 per cent) for whom lack of finance was a definite hindrance to the full use of science and technology. The 14 per cent included those firms which were unwilling to accept the conditions on which they could have raised fresh money. The frustrated minority included a high proportion of progressive and rapidly expanding firms—typically firms which were 'outgrowing their strength'; at a time of high taxation they could not retain enough profit to finance their own expansion, and they were not yet of a size and age to find it easy to raise fresh capital from outside. Our general conclusion was that 'there is some hindrance to the adoption of new scientific and technical ideas due to the natural difficulty of providing finance, with independence, for new, young or small firms'.[1]

There is a presumption that, with the increasing severity of the 'credit squeeze', these frustrations may have become worse in the period 1956–8. On reviewing our sample, however, we found that the *additional* firms which appeared from their financial position to have actual or potential difficulties in raising money were too few to justify comparisons between the different periods. We therefore offer no evidence on this matter.

We have had access to other evidence[2] which shows that in the period 1948–53 the fastest-growing public companies with Stock Exchange quotations, achieving an increase in their net assets of over 100 per cent during the period, could finance only half of their net investment from their own saving, and relied heavily on the capital market. Nevertheless, on the average they *improved* their liquidity position over the period, which does not suggest a *general* difficulty in raising money. The same evidence shows that larger companies were able to achieve more investment than smaller companies, and to raise more capital, in proportion to their size. These facts seem consistent with our belief that since the War the frustration of innovation by shortage of finance has been occasional rather than general, but may have been important in small, young, or rapidly growing progressive firms.

---

[1] *Industry and Technical Progress*, p. 147.
[2] To be published by the Cambridge University Press on behalf of the National Institute for Economic and Social Research, under the title *Studies in Company Finance*.

The last of our main questions relates to the *unconsidered* projects. It must be expected that, in the best of worlds, *some* good projects will be left unconsidered; for there are too many possibilities of useful work to make it certain that all can be reviewed, and where preliminary research and development is required, what are later seen to be good projects can easily be overlooked. Where, however, an industry (or a country), rather than just a single firm, persistently overlooks good projects we can expect to find that the industry or country concerned is inefficient—that it organizes its research and development badly or has too little of it, or that it is forced to operate in an unfavourable environment, caused by such things as political instability, or a scarcity of capital, or a shortage of scientific and technical manpower. We believe that in Britain there is an unreasonably high ratio of unconsidered projects, due to poor organization of research and development, to there being too little of it in private industry, and to a shortage of trained men and women.

Research and development should be conceived as part of a group of inter-related functions in the firm. Every firm has to produce and to sell; the function of research and development arises from new problems in production and selling, and from new possibilities of production created by developments elsewhere. Such things as changes in materials; pressure from customers for new qualities and types of product; rising competition which directs attention to price, and thus to cost, reduction; changes in relative prices of labour, materials, and capital—these are the new problems in production and selling. Often the production staff lacks the skill or the time to solve these problems, and a special department is created for the purpose. In this sense, the function of research and development derives directly from the problems of producing and selling.

The link may seem less obvious when new possibilities of production emerge from research and development. But there is no point in researching into or designing or developing new things if they cannot be sold at a price, and in a quantity, which would justify the investment in them, or if they would require a form or scale of production beyond the technical and financial resources of the firm. Thus unless research, design, and development efforts are closely related to the activities of production, sales, and finance they may be wasted. Without this close relation, a research or development department may indeed find it difficult to secure the adoption even of worthwhile inventions; for there will be many problems competing for the attention of those concerned with producing and selling the firm's output, and the 'back-room boys' will not obtain a share of that attention unless they know how to present their ideas in an appropriate and relevant manner.

Research and development in fact, is a management technique which needs to be considered as an integral part of the whole activity of the firm. Failure to realize this may lead to good projects being unconsidered, and poor projects getting an undue priority. In addition to poor organization, there is too little research and development, and too little attention to the drawing in and sifting of relevant technical information; this is due partly to the shortage of trained men and women, and partly to the prevalence of parochialism. The two are, of course, inter-related. The shortage of trained men and women is a sign of a growing consciousness of the way opportunities for innovation can be created or utilized by taking thought in appropriate ways. With the growth of that consciousness, failure to invest in worthwhile innovation will become less serious.

Seven   Predictions—true and false

In the last two chapters we have been analysing some of the reasons which lead to the acceptance or rejection of investment proposals, and in these chapters we have necessarily referred to the problem of uncertainty. Also, in order to set the stage on which our later discussion could proceed, we made in Chapter III a general and theoretical analysis of the likely effects of uncertainty. The subject is, however, so important to an understanding of the determinants of investment that we devote this further chapter to an examination of the evidence provided by our case-studies on the reaction of firms to uncertainty.

In this context, however, we prefer to classify the problem as one of 'prediction'; that is to say, we shall be interested in those *actions* of firms by which they navigate in the darkness and fog which surround the future. Our terms of reference will be slightly wider than in Chapter III, for we shall be interested not only in the inherent and uninsurable uncertainties of the future, but also in its assessable risks, and in the darkness caused by the failure of management to provide itself with available information. The general analysis of Chapter III stands, however; the range, difficulty, and importance of prediction vary greatly, both according to the type and attitude of the firm and according to the type of situation with which it is faced; and there are various ways in which prediction can be made easier, or the need for it avoided.[1]

The evidence from the firms we have visited will be used in this chapter first to give an idea of the effectiveness of the predictions actually made; this will yield a general measure of the problem. Then we shall classify the nature of the forecasts so as to show what types of prediction are most frequently required. Next we shall say a little about the methods of forecasting used by the firms; and finally, we shall link the discussion to the important problem of fluctuations in investment.

We have made a special study of prediction in a few firms which

[1] See p. 17–22.

produce estimates of the expected and actual yield on capital investment. Some of these firms have also given details of the expected and
actual cost of their investment projects, and have told us why the
yield and the cost have diverged from what was expected. The projects included some which were mainly extension rather than innovation, but there is probably a substantial element of improvement
in the extensions. The details are naturally confidential, and we are
therefore only able to summarize them, as follows:

(*a*) The *expected* return on the capital projects covered varied very
widely, from 4 to 46 per cent. This variation we have analysed
further in Chapter V.

(*b*) The *actual* return varied still more widely, from nil or a loss to
52 per cent. The difference between actual and expected return was
50 per cent of the expected return or more in nearly three-quarters
of the cases; it exceeded 100 per cent (i.e. there was in fact either a
loss or a profit more than double what was expected) in over a
quarter of the cases. In interpreting these figures it must be remembered that the 'actual' yield from recent investment projects is obtained from data relating to a short period; it is *possible* that the
long-run yield might be closer to expectation.

(*c*) The correlation between estimated and actual yield was low,
only 0·13. The two regression coefficients were small, 0·20 and 0·09.
This underlines the necessity of explaining investment behaviour in
terms of what the firm expects, and not in terms of what actually
happens.

(*d*) In general, over-estimation and under-estimation of yield
were about equally likely in the cases studied. But in particular
companies there were cases both of a general tendency to over-estimate
and a general tendency to under-estimate yields; this is probably
due in part to lack of experience at the time when the estimates were
made, and in part to the tendency of some companies to estimate
'hopefully' and others to estimate 'conservatively' (see p. 74–5).
There was also some evidence of a tendency to under-estimate yields
for investments completed in the early 1950's, and to over-estimate
them for those completed after mid-1955; in other words, firms did
not fully foresee a change in trading conditions.

(*e*) The reasons for the difference between expected and actual
return are difficult to analyse, because several (working in the same
or different directions) may have been operating together to produce
the observed divergence. Ignoring the offsetting reasons (i.e. those
which by themselves would produce a divergence in a direction

different from that actually observed), and counting where necessary several reasons for a particular case, we obtain the rough classification given below.

The importance of changes in demand can be seen. Many of these were changes in the demand for an intermediate product, deriving from a change in the nature of, or the demand for, some final products of other industries. Given the long period which must often elapse between the final decision to go ahead with a new plant and the sale of its first product, it is clearly unreasonable to expect many of these complex changes in demand to be foreseen; market research is not an answer to everything.

Reasons	Percentage distribution of reasons where yield was—		
	better than expected	worse than expected	All cases
Unforeseen changes of demand, or changes in price of competing product	50	61	57
Cost of investment different from estimate	17	28	23
Technical possibilities of investment not correctly foreseen	33	11	20
	100	100	100

(*f*) The relation between expected and actual cost for investment projects varies from company to company. Some companies persistently under-estimate the cost of their projects—sometimes, perhaps, because the difficulties cannot be foreseen, but probably more often because of careless forecasting of constructional price trends and inadequate budgetary control, or because they have chosen to make no allowance for inflation in their estimates. Other companies obtain a very close agreement with estimates—errors of less than 2 per cent being common. One large firm comments that overspending in excess of 10 per cent occurs in fewer than 1 per cent of their projects.

The evidence from this special study of prediction must not be taken as necessarily representative. The assessment of projects in definite quantitative terms is the exception rather than the rule, and the experience of firms which do not quantify their decisions might be different. Furthermore, our examples necessarily relate to easily identifiable items of investment such as a new works or a new plant. The estimation of the yield of a lesser improvement is more difficult and speculative. One managing director, when asked for more precise details of forecast and actual yields, replied: 'This is a most interesting subject, but I think you will have to go to the big boys, with better organized statistical departments than our own, to get worthwhile information.' Actually our examples include some provided by small firms, but the point which the managing director was trying to make was that, if the innovation is not embodied in a whole new works or a new plant, then a good deal of statistical inference is required for a worthwhile estimate of actual yield. An improved piece of equipment may, for example, be associated with improved management arrangements. What will any improvement of profit be due to? Even if the improved management is induced by the technical change, it may well have been a great advantage in any case; and the technical innovation may only have influenced the *timing* of the management change.

Nor must we forget the subjective nature of some of the estimates. One business man comments: 'It is our experience that the relation of estimate to actual is very much a reflection of the temperament of the people concerned, for, whatever steps may be taken by disinterested and (let us hope) scientifically minded experts to assist in preparing these estimates, in the last event they depend upon the judgement of those who are responsible for the various projects. . . . To the extent that estimates cannot be made accurately and have to depend on judgement, then the relationship between estimate and "actual" will reflect the quality of that judgement, and that in turn will reflect the quality and temperament of the man himself. . . .'[1]

The problem of prediction varies with the type of firm and with the nature of the situation with which it is faced. We have therefore, after examining the results of our case-studies, formed a rough classification of types of situation and of prediction, in order to see which are most important. We start with the cases of least complexity, where the element of prediction must seem trivial to the firm concerned, and we then move to cases of greater complexity.

(i) A firm making satisfactory profits may decide that parts of its equipment are worn out, since the machines can no longer maintain output at the required level or quality. If the machines are 'fully depreciated', the purchase of improved and fully tested machines will not seem to require the explicit prediction of anything, but simply a decision to stay in business, with an implicit long-range prediction

[1] Part of this comment was used in a different context on p. 53.

that it will be a worthwhile activity. In some cases the firm may have no choice about the innovation; for instance, the firm supplying the machine may have developed and tested new types, and discontinued production of the old.

(ii) A firm making high profits may have excess orders. It may judge that output could be increased if a particular part of the process could be altered; and there may be successful research or development work designed to widen the bottleneck. In this case, so long as the new process is not out of scale with the rest of the processes, and so long as the cost is reasonable in relation to the prospective increases of output, the investment in the new process will seem 'obviously sensible'. Once again, there will not seem to be a need to predict the future course of events except in a general and short-term sense—namely, that the excess demand is not monetary. Because the investment is induced by an actual pressure of demand the element of risk will seem small.

(iii) There may be a combination of cases (i) and (ii) in which the investment in an innovation involves both replacement and a general increase in capacity. A good example of this was the post-war introduction of the tunnel oven in the pottery industry.[1] Before the War there was a substantial element of uncertainty about the technical performance of tunnel ovens, and the prediction of technical performance was the great problem in deciding to invest in this innovation. But by the end of the War the technical performance was fairly well known, and to justify an investment in replacing old ovens by the new type it was only necessary to make a general prediction that the national population and product would increase and that the rate of substitution through time between glass or plastics and pottery would be small. This prediction was necessary because the minimum size of tunnel ovens is large; they are not suited to a small and variable trade. Another example discussed in *Industry and Technical Progress* (pp. 220–9) is jute, and in this industry it was necessary to predict the future maintenance and effects of Government promises to protect the industry. Given an enlarged and protected market, both replacement of old machines and provision of new capacity appeared sensible. A comment by one manufacturer makes the point: 'In our case, having decided in 1949 to stay in the industry, the necessary investment had to follow. The decision was based largely on promises by successive governments that modernization would be supported by protection from Asiatic competition.'

[1] See *Industry and Technical Progress*, pp. 201–13.

We will say more about this form of prediction when we consider below the substitutes for explicit prediction.

In more complex cases the innovation depends less on a passive reaction to market pressures or to the innovation of others, and more on a decision to create a new technology or to prepare for a market change predicted for the future. These we now discuss.

(iv) First let us consider cases involving an increase in demand, but of a more complex and uncertain kind than the excess of current orders discussed in (ii). A firm might, for example, predict that there will be free trade with Europe within the next five years; or it might predict that real income per head will increase and that the consequent new expenditure pattern can be deduced from United States experience; or it might predict that a customer industry will grow at a particular rate, and that by producing components for that industry it will itself be able to grow quickly; or it might predict from present trends of technical development in other industries that there will be a big increase in the demand for its products during the next ten years.

An example of a complex demand prediction of this kind is provided by the petrochemicals industry, where capacity to produce of many kinds is being laid down well ahead of present demand. The confidence of prediction is reflected in the following passages:[1]

Before World War II, petroleum chemicals were not produced commercially in the United Kingdom. In 1947 12,000 tons were produced, and, ten years later, output had risen to 430,000 tons. Within another three years this last figure will have more than doubled and, by 1975, annual production may be some $2\frac{1}{2}$ million tons.'

The research and development, which has progressed for years in oil company laboratories and a great many other institutions, has started an industry whose rapid growth in the past decade has been a phenomenon of post-war commerce. Its products, compared with the pre-war plastics industry, whose raw materials were largely from animal or vegetable sources and whose wares seldom had any great virtue other then cheapness, are almost unlimited. They often improve a similar natural substance and invent what Nature forgot.

Oil is a fabulous source of industrial raw materials. Already it can supply the basis of an almost countless range of chemical compounds. The range will be extended almost beyond belief by the time that atomic power is efficiently providing most of our energy needs.

[1] From *Esso Magazine*, Winter 1957/8, pp. 3, 4.

Examples of the same kind of confidence can be found in firms producing components for the oil industry or for the atomic-energy programme. But assurance about the long-term trend is not a reliable guide to profitable investment, as we can see from the recent failure of oil demand to reach predicted levels, After the War, some industries made investments in new and improved capacity which proved unprofitable, because of failure to develop expected large markets in particular regions. Thus one pottery firm no longer uses a multi-headed automatic plate-making machine which it developed and built in the hope of supplying a mass market in Europe. Another firm built a remarkable automatic factory to assemble cheap radios for mass sale in China; but they failed to predict the collapse of the Nationalist Government.

The uncertainty of investment depends both on the uncertainty of predictions and on the way in which predictions are used. Forecasts of the actions of single firms, or of small numbers of firms, are likely to be much more uncertain than broad forecasts of national aggregates. It requires no great courage to reach the conclusion that national income is likely to increase 1 or 2 per cent per year. Even such broad forecasts are likely to take the form of a range of possibilities: to say '1 or 2 per cent' is reasonable, while to say simply '2 per cent' is rash. If the 'conservative' end of range of prediction is used as a basis for investment, the uncertainty of the investment will be lower than if there is a reliance on bolder possibilities. Thus a firm might feel confident that the number of cars in use in a country will increase by 5–10 per cent in three years; but there will be a much smaller sense of uncertainty if the lower estimate is used as the basis for investment plans.

(v) The decision to 'create a new technology'—that is, to attempt a whole series of inter-related changes of process which will together constitute something which is technically quite new—may or may not require an increase in demand to yield a successful outcome. If the existing demand is sufficient, the main elements in the prediction are the technical performance of the new process and the reactions of management and labour to the new situation.

A prediction about performance may have to be based on experience with small-scale models or with full-scale prototypes under special conditions. The more novel the new process, the greater the difficulty of predicting normal running cost, maintenance cost, and useful life. Normal running cost will depend on the reaction of operatives and supervisors to the new process or the new machines, and it will therefore be necessary to predict the strength of objection to the new procedures, the possibility of overcoming that objection, and the time it will take to create new working arrangements.

A tragic example of the difficulty of predicting the useful life of equipment was provided by the original Comet jet airliner, whose failure was due to lack of technical and theoretical knowledge about fatigue in structures. The research which lay behind the Comet was considered to be a model of its kind, and yet it led to a wrong prediction of useful life. An example of wrong prediction in the other direction is provided by the atomic-energy programme, whose economic justification is now much stronger than when it was first started. This is because technical changes, such as increases in the fuel-element surface temperature and in the pressure of the heat-transfer gas, have over a short period roughly doubled the amount of heat extracted from each ton of uranium. With this change and with the building of larger reactors, the capital cost per kilowatt of output has been substantially reduced. The useful life and the maintenance cost of atomic power stations are, however, still unknown; they may prove to be more or less favourable than expected.

(vi) Finally, some ventures involve both a decision to make great technical change and a complex forecast of demand. Here the element of uncertainty is likely to be greatest and the need for explicit prediction most pressing. Thus an aircraft firm may predict a considerable growth of demand for air travel, a desire for faster travel, and a preference for higher speed rather than lower fares. On this basis it may design a radically new type of aircraft. The number of unknowns in this form of prediction must be large and the degree of unresolvable uncertainty very great.

This analysis of the types of forecast to be made suggests that we should return to the distinction[1] between *passive* decisions (types (i), (ii), and (iii))—in which the firm is making innovations under pressure of a need to replace worn-out machinery or to satisfy orders—and *active* decisions (types (iv), (v), and (vi)), which involve a reaching out after new markets or new techniques. Our case-study material (covering 250 cases of innovation supplied by 116 firms) certainly under-represents innovations of type (i)—that is to say, those introduced in the course of normal replacement. A classification of the material therefore gives information mainly about types (ii) to (vi). As mentioned on p. 42, 60 per cent of the innovations fell in the 'active' category, but two-thirds of these (40 per cent of the whole)

[1] See pp. 41–2 above.

were in category (iv), in which the pressure from technical innovation was relatively unimportant, and the decisions were based on a general prediction that 'demand will increase' or that 'the potential market is large'. Cases of type (vi), where the sense of uncertainty would be greatest, were rare (5 per cent of the whole). Of the 40 per cent of innovations following 'passive' decisions, two-thirds (i.e. about a quarter of the whole) were of type (iii)—that is to say, they were induced by excess demand (and thus entailed an increase in output), but a need for replacement also existed.

It appears that in the post-war period which we have studied the extent of grave uncertainty, involving serious efforts of prediction, was usually small. Almost 80 per cent of the cases of investment in innovation studied were either passive or involved prediction only of a vague and general kind, and this percentage would be further increased if there were a fuller coverage of 'replacement' cases of type (i). The main reason for the 'unimportance of uncertainty' was the extent to which firms were drawn into innovation by excess demand, or short supply, or the enterprise of suppliers of plant and machinery; it was also due in part to the use of research and development to reduce or eliminate technical uncertainties. Without this last factor type (iv) would have been less predominant.

The period was, in fact, one of optimism, in which innovation moved forward under the pressure of immediate demand or of generally held hopes about the future. This confirms our analysis on pp. 21–3: despite the great uncertainty necessarily surrounding the future, the *sense* of uncertainty need not be acute at all times. The situation we describe may well have changed since our case-studies were made.

Only a small number of firms in our sample make their investment decisions in the light of a quantitative forecast of the relation between revenues and costs. In view of the predominant types of investment (as analysed above), this is not surprising. However, this is not the only reason. A high proportion of firms do not use management techniques which would enable them to make reasonable forecasts.

Why do some firms go in for formal and quantitative predictions, while others are content with vague 'hunches'? Three factors seem to us important: size, the importance of research and development, and the extent of investment of type (vi), which involves both technical and market risks. As a firm gets larger its management structure becomes more complex; there is more 'paper work', and what were formerly guesses in the Managing Director's mind assume the respectability of recorded 'estimates' passed from department to department. The Managing Director can convince himself by means of an unformed feeling that a particular course is hopeful; but if the Research Director has to win over the Finance Director by means of a proposal in writing, there will be a tendency to put in figures. It is not enough to write a memorandum saying, 'I think this is a good idea'; its goodness must be given an apparent precision by recording figures of expected yield or of 'pay-off period'.

The growth of a research and development department leads to an increase in the number of potential investment projects brought under review; and this before long leads to a growth of interest in the problem of ranking them in order of merit. With the growth of research there may also go an increased interest in the large technical changes which are involved in investments of type (vi). The use of a new technique to produce goods for new markets, created by large changes in production elsewhere, sometimes faces firms with a choice of 'going in big' or not going in at all. It is not possible to creep up on the problem by making a small and tentative investment first. Where these big decisions have to be made, quantitative estimates are often an indispensible guide to clarity of thought.

On the other hand, there is no incentive to make formal predictions where a firm is pulled into innovation by the tension of excess demand, or pushed by the need to overcome shortages. Nor will there be much need for sophisticated prediction when a supplier offers a machine to replace existing labour; the firm's attitude is then determined by some general rule such as the following: 'One of our Research Associations gives as an approximate guide that an expenditure on a machine of £1,500 to £2,000 is justified if this enables the labour force to be reduced by one employee.' A firm which can make a gradual approach to a problem by tentative experiment may never need formal predictions about the future. A firm which feels that it must, as a condition of survival, adopt the latest techniques, may do so without careful calculation of the results.

The methods by which firms make formal predictions of the future vary; some examples are given in the next chapter. There are differences in the extent to which variables are taken into account. Thus some firms use current prices, wages, and other factor costs to make their forecasts, on the assumption that these will have the same proportionate variations. But where (as in three cases in the sample) long-term budgeting is considered a condition of the maximum use of resources, the cash position is of considerable significance and in this case predictions about the *actual* movements of prices and factor costs are required.

There are, as we have seen, different ways of calculating yield. In several of our cases the yield is calculated on the fixed investment *before* making provision for working capital, even though working-capital needs are considerable. Some firms calculate the yield before tax, though those which think in terms of a 'pay-off period' are implicitly calculating a yield after tax payments.

Many firms do not make calculations of yield. As we have seen, they may isolate one factor for attention, and they will then generally assume an absence of change in the others. But firms which do not formulate expectations generally have a vaguer idea of the trend of the market, and their forecasts are less sensitive to *signs* of a change in trend and more sensitive to an *actual* change. On the other hand, in so far as they maintain a higher liquidity ratio, their investment may be less sensitive to a decline in expected profits than in the case of firms that plan farther ahead.

Forecasts are often sensitive to the known actions of competitors. Thus a firm may have decided against a particular project, or made a 'not-yet' decision. It may have decided: (*a*) that the project is too low in the queue to be taken this year; or (*b*) that the time is not yet ripe—that though the project looks good there is insufficient information about technical possibilities or about how the market would receive the output; or (*c*) that though the idea is a good one the firm lacks the key staff that would ensure its success; or (*d*) that the project is too big, or too small, or 'not in our line of business'. In all these cases knowledge that a competitor has made a different decision may be sufficient to induce a change of mind—either a rational decision to change, because of the situation created by the action of the competitor, or a sheep-like revision of expectation.

In the process of making predictions in figures, there is generally a strong tendency for the statistical limits of the forecast to be forgotten. Ranges of possibility are replaced by definite figures; an outcome which was first considered as the most likely among many possibilities is treated as though it were the only possible outcome. It is, however, difficult to assess the importance of this translation of doubt into certainty, for (especially in some of the larger firms) successive estimators tend to put in contingency allowances, often of unspecified size, and inserted in ignorance of the contingency allowances already implicit in the forecasts received from others. In three of our case-studies research and production departments add such large items for contingencies that no programmes appear worthwhile until the investment committee forces these departments to reveal the extent of their hidden allowances. On the other hand, predictions by sales departments of the value of sales are frequently thought to be over-optimistic. It is difficult to tell whether they actually *are* over-optimistic; but they lack the caution which is felt to be necessary by estimators in other departments.

To sum up—methods of forecasting vary all the way from vague hunches to precise and elaborate statistical estimates; but the quality of an estimate is not measured by its precision, which may be much more apparent than real. Indeed, an apparently precise estimate in some cases conceals the truth of the situation, which is that a wide range of possible outcomes exists; it may be that the firm concerned should be thinking first of all of flexibility in meeting these varied possibilities, and not of wagering all on a single choice.

The graph of an economic variable, such as the output or price of a product, or the profits of the industry which makes it, is frequently highly irregular. There may be a discernible long-term trend, but short-term movements may make it difficult to decide whether or not the trend is changing its shape or direction. Now in so far as investments is based on formal predictions, those predictions are likely to be based in part on past experience and to assume the continuance of past trends—with the exception, already noted, that some companies assumed fixed prices and wages in making their forecasts. Therefore when trends do change, the belated discovery of the change may produce sudden and violent revisions of investment plans.

In principle, the man who does *not* quantify his estimates could by the exercise of a sensitive 'feel of the situation' avoid some of the errors committed by those who hold to the false security of figures. But such is the infectious power of optimism and pessimism that it is likely that investment decisions based on hunches will similarly be subject to violent revision. In mid-1929 Mr Bernard Baruch said in an interview, 'the economic condition of the world seems on the verge of a great forward movement'; in the autumn of that year Professor Irving Fisher thought that 'stock prices have reached what looks like a permanently high plateau'; in November the Harvard Economic Society went on record that 'a severe depression like that of 1920–21 is outside the range of probability'.[1] But the actual

---

[1] Quoted in J. K. Galbraith, *The Great Crash*, Hamish Hamilton, 1955.

downturn of business activity was in June 1929, and the panic on Wall Street began on October 24th. Between June and November many business men must have been making real, as well as financial, investment decisions which in retrospect were seen to be ill-founded.

The main influences (other than the supply of outside capital) by which fluctuations in investment in innovations may be caused are—

(a) changes in the supply of investment projects, whether created within or outside the firm;
(b) changes in the length of the queue of orders;
(c) changes in profits;
(d) changes in the trend of the growth of markets;
(e) competitive pressure.

These influences are, of course, interrelated, but a particular one may be the first to press itself upon the attention of the firm. There is no reason to expect a smooth supply of investment projects, though with the growth of effective research and development the supply is likely to be smoother. We have found cases in which projects of lower priority are 'put on the shelf', to be brought out in slack times; but this method of equalizing the flow of new projects is perhaps only likely to be used under conditions of competitive pressure. The flow of new projects is necessarily highly irregular if the firm is very small.

Excess demand has been an important cause of investment in innovation. It has led to investment in devices for the easing of shortages—whether of labour, of materials, or of equipment which has become out of balance with the rest of the productive process. Excess demand has also, as we have seen, lessened the sense of uncertainty in predicting the success of a venture. A reduction in a very long queue may have little effect on investment—it does not matter much if an order book is four years or three years long. But, at a certain stage, an easing or disappearance of excess demand is liable to cause a considerable change in investment.

Sensitivity to a fall in profit is likely to be important in small firms, or in large firms with a high ratio of investment to assets, where the firm has budgeted for the financing of its investment from profits which are not in fact achieved. At the very least, such a fall in profits is likely to bring a delay, while real and financial plans are being thought out again. A rise of profits takes its effect only if it is considered to be evidence of strong demand or of future growth, or if it induces in those who make decisions a warm glow of optimism.

Fluctuations of profits in firms with a low ratio of investment to assets are not of themselves of great importance in inducing changes of investment, though they may again be considered as evidence of other changes.

An established change in the trend of the growth of markets, in either direction, is an important influence; and since (for the reasons stated above) realization of the change is liable to come late, the change of policy may be considerable. Competitive pressure makes itself felt, not only in order books and profit margins, but in news or rumours that competitors are installing new equipment. This led, for instance, to a keen competition by the motor-car industry to obtain the use of scarce capacity in the machine-tool firms which could produce transfer machines.

Broadly speaking, the influences causing fluctuations in the *desire* to invest seem to us to have been more important than those causing fluctuations in the *ability* to invest. The refusal of capital can, of course, hold up large projects; there is the important field of State-controlled industries, in which the total of investment is subject to central direction; in a few marginal cases, high interest rates may tip the balance towards rejection, or low interest rates towards acceptance. But such influences are not typically important in the general run of medium and small investment projects in private industry—the day-to-day and piecemeal improvement of products, processes, and methods. Where the desire to invest in new techniques or products has persisted, firms have shown remarkable ingenuity in finding capital, or self-control in saving it. Where the desire has been weak, cheap and easy money has seldom proved a sufficient stimulus to action.

Eight Some examples from the case-studies

In this chapter we give a few examples of the process of investment. We have included firms from craft, engineering, and modern industries; firms that have had little or much trouble in financing what they thought to be desirable levels of investment; and firms that have been 'passive' or 'active' in their investment policy.

(a) FIRM OF MEDIUM GROWTH-RATE IN A TRADITIONAL INDUSTRY

In the industry research activity is of recent growth and is concentrated mainly in the Research Association. There have been substantial changes in production technique since the War, and there are technical opportunities for considerable further change. In the early post-war period output expanded rapidly, but the high growth rate was not maintained. The industry is now expected to grow slowly and intermittently, because of the increasing number of substitutes, and the growth of production overseas.

The company in this study is of medium size, though large in relation to the average size of firm in the industry. It is a leader in production techniques. Since the War, output per head has increased at three times the rate for the industry as a whole. The increase in production is, however, near the average rate for the industry. Quite early in the post-war boom, the firm predicted that the expansion would not last. It decided to concentrate on reducing cost and improving quality. Any increase of output is a consequence of better production flow.

In investment policy there is a great stress on long-term stability. Since the War all pre-war machinery has been replaced. This is a consequence of the basic policy of reducing cost and improving quality, rather than expanding output. The incentives to improve efficiency were: (i) the expected rise in labour cost (which is a high proportion of total cost); (ii) the competition from substitute materials; and (iii) greater competition in foreign markets, which take two-thirds of the firm's output.

78

In the 1930's there was thought to be a shortage of profitable innovations. Since then there has been an aggressive policy of finding or creating investment opportunities. The development of research-association activities has increased knowledge of materials and manufacturing processes. In company (a) a research department, capable of using and developing this knowledge, and an engineering department, with the job of developing new production techniques (or of copying practice in other industries), have been set up. The company also uses consultants for assessing immediate as well as long-term technical and market trends. In addition, it has purchased operating plant in North America, which helps to ensure that it has very good information about technical and marketing developments in the United States.

Costing of existing processes is highly developed and, within limits explained below, prospective yields on capital expenditure are calculated. The company has plans extending into the future, but it has had no need to develop a capital budget—all development since the War has been financed out of profits, leaving large reserves untouched.

In judging whether investment in a new product or a new process is worth while the firm sets a standard of at least 20 per cent gross yield on the fixed investment. The existence of such a standard, however, does not in itself tell us a great deal about the investment process in the firm. Before we can judge the significance of this standard we need to know whether mere guesses or reasoned estimates are the basis of yield calculation, how far competitive pressure forces the firm to act without reference to its standard (for instance, in changing its products), and how far the firm goes in applying its standard even apart from competitive pressure.

Given that the firm has a highly developed system of costing and estimating, the extent to which it bases its yield calculations on guesses rather than on reasoned estimates depends on the extent to which its innovation is 'active' rather than 'passive', in the sense defined in Chapter Five. Company (a) is certainly not just pushed into innovation by excess demand or by the action of suppliers. Its own contribution to technical development is small, but it is well organized to pull in new technical possibilities from a variety of sources. The firm's own 'research and development' work is short term; it is skilled in finding and identifying process developments that are practically ready for use. Furthermore, from the nature of the production process, it is usually possible to 'creep up' on a risky project by trying it out on a small scale. In such a case, either the calculation is based on a solid estimate rather than a guess, or the size of the risky investment is kept small.

There have been cases where the firm has been forced to invest defensively—where it has taken the attitude that it is forced by competition to invest in a new product or process. Such directly defensive investment has been rare. There are, however, certain projects in which the firm has not been investing defensively, but where the yield has not been calculated. Thus, if a particular form of finish is expected to become impossible with existing methods because of the shortage of skilled labour, new equipment may be put in for this purpose. There may be no saving in cost, but the project would be undertaken if there was a market demand which the firm wants to meet. There are also pieces of investment which are non-specific, for example, trucks for conveyance and storage. Here there is a saving in labour, a saving in damage to moulds and dies, and the new method makes it possible to carry a big stock of moulds and dies. In this way, orders can be dealt with while maintaining the correct flow of production. This is regarded as essential to profitable trading in markets which are widely varying. It would have been possible to make a rough calculation of yield, but as there was a lot of cost-work needed, and as it would have been necessary to make guesses about how much longer the moulds would last, no detailed calculation was in fact made; all rough estimates pointed in the same direction, and a decision to proceed was made. Such projects are, however, probably less than one-third of investment by value.

In replacing machinery, the procedure is rather different; for small replacements the firm does not bother to make an explicit calculation; for larger expenditure it does. Immediately after the War, however, it decided to buy process machinery without making calculations of yield. The money was available, but not the labour, and machinery was the only way to get production increased. Product prices were in fact good, and if a calculation had been made the probable yield would have been high.

In calculations of yield the present state of profits seems to have exercised a significant influence on the confidence or pessimism of the forecast only with projects that are risky because of inadequate technical knowledge. There, in the balancing of optimistic against pessimistic estimates, the scales are tipped towards the latter when current profits are low. Apart from this, investment is not sensitive to short-term market changes. In the situation that we have described this is not surprising.

(b) FIRM OF LOW GROWTH-RATE IN ENGINEERING

This company, in the 'engineering' sector of industry, makes machines for firms in the 'traditional' sector, which is not likely to have a high growth rate. Until recently, it could be regarded as large, but now, after business reverses due to changes overseas, it is in the medium-size group.

In the six years following 1948 net tangible assets increased by one-third and trading profits by a little over 10 per cent. In the following years there was a very sharp fall in profits, and then losses. The company relied heavily on overseas markets for the sale of its equipment, the design of which had changed little for a generation or more. Due to currency difficulties and to manufacture overseas the traditional overseas markets almost disappeared in 1954. The company is being reorganized, and net tangible assets are now one-half the level of 1948.

The attitude of the company to investment has changed substantially. Before the War there was no investment in innovation. The company produced a wide range of machines, waited for customers to suggest any improvements, and pursued a conservative policy on replacement of equipment, whether of machine tools, foundry equipment, or buildings. In consequence, at the end of the War the company had poor buildings, obsolete equipment, and was unprogressive in design and development.

After the War there was an urge to re-equip and to design and develop new machines. This urge was related to competition from more youthful and better-equipped rivals, to change in membership of the Board, and to signs of new life in the traditional industries for which the machinery is produced. Over £1 m. was spent on re-equipment, and of this two-thirds was financed from reserves. The re-investment programme reached its peak, and outstanding capital commitments fell away sharply, before the set-back in sales.

Expenditure and commitments on buildings, plant, and equipment have fallen further since the decline in sales, but reorganization has included considerable redesign and development work on old lines of product and also a search for new products. Capital-expenditure plans (but so far not commitments) are now rising again to the pre-1954 level.

Prior to 1945 there was very little attention given to investigating and evaluating potential innovations. Equipment was replaced when it was worn out, and products were only altered or adapted to customer specification. After the War it was decided to get the factory up to date and to institute 'design and development' work, in order to improve the machines produced without waiting for suggestions and pressure from customers. Getting the factory up to date was relatively the simpler task, involving co-operation with suppliers of up-to-date equipment, whether foundry plant or machine tools. This capital-expenditure programme was not based on calculations of profitability, except in the general engineering sense that 'this piece of equipment was the best adapted for that type of work'. There was pressure from an 'up-to-date' competitor, and it was assumed that profits would follow modernization. Profits were good, and it was easy to raise new capital equal to about one-third of the cost of the projected capital expenditure.

The re-design of the firm's machines and the introduction of new products was seen as a longer-term problem, and for this purpose a re-design and development unit was created. This was small (0·5 per cent of the labour employed), and its activity was divided between reconsidering the function and design of traditional products and designing quite new types of engineering products—one of which had arisen as a result of problems in the firm's own foundry operation. The size and tempo of this work was such that the new design and development unit would not quickly exert a strong pressure to innovate. At any rate, the re-design and development had not gone far before the recession in 1954.

Because of the great change in the market situation a radical change in procedure became a condition of survival. It was decided that the market for traditional products would decline, that an effort must be made to find profitable new items which could be produced as far as possible with existing equipment, and that, as the company's financial position is precarious, efforts should also be made to buy rights to produce items of proved design with a known demand. Investment is now related to these policy decisions.

Investment at present being undertaken falls into the following categories:

(i) unavoidable replacement;
(ii) expenditure on plant required to extend the range of products;
(iii) capital investment needed for particular new products to be

produced on contract, usually for a minimum period or a minimum quantity;

(iv) investment in connexion with new products emanating from the design and development department.

For replacement of equipment the department concerned must produce evidence that the machine is no longer economic. In one case noted, the rate-fixing department provided both the incentive to replace and the details of the appropriate new machine.

In the second category the cost and performance of the new plant are now investigated and, as the plant is usually of a standard type, such information is readily available. But the main consideration which counts in evaluating the proposition is that if the new-type product is to be made the plant *must* be purchased. There is evidence of varying attention to cost-revenue considerations. Where members of the Board doubt the necessity of some new piece of equipment more attention is given to financial evaluation.

In the third category evaluation is done by a small committee composed of the sales, technical, and financial directors. On the technical side this evaluation is fairly detailed. On the market side neither investigation nor evaluation is close. Sales forecasting is in fact still 'conspicuous by its absence', though the need for it is now recognized.

In the fourth category investigation and evaluation are becoming more sophisticated. The re-design of a machine is undertaken in relation to a general analysis of function, an analysis of all past known faults of operation and user's complaints, and the testing of a prototype in a customer's plant. It is felt that the incorporation of significant improvements should then ensure its sale. With a newer product, if it is a fairly expensive one and involves a large number of bought-in parts and expensive dies, the process of investigation and evaluation is now extended to a detailed survey of the potential markets.

The extent of explicit forecasting involved in investment decisions has been small. Until quite recently forecasting had not gone much beyond such very general judgements as that 'unless the firm modernized it would not be able to withstand competition', or that 'the state of the market would ensure profits if the firm got up to date'. The absence of planning was due to the fact that the firm was known throughout the world, produced to order, and relied on salesmen in various parts of the world to get the orders which would keep the factory going.

The firm was forced to pay more attention to planning by the growth of competition and the (partly consequent) desire to diversify. However, the old procedures were not greatly changed until losses forced re-organization and a more obvious need to justify capital expenditure. In the context of loss on operations the uncertain nature of implicit forecasts became more obvious. This has led to an attempt to reduce uncertainty by more attention to building and testing prototypes and to market research. For the time being also there is a greater stress on getting the rights to manufacture a new machine proved in (say) another country, rather than on taking a chance with a new machine from the firm's own designs.

It is clear from the earlier account of procedures for investigating and evaluating investment opportunities that the firm has no definite rules for judging the worthwhileness of investment. Some investments, as we have already mentioned, proceeds from a policy decision to extend the general range of output. Usually there is no explicit consideration of the return on capital, just that 'if we are to make (so and so) we must have this type of plant'.

For investment required for certain specific new products, however, the firm now requires reasonable paper evidence of a return on capital, as well as an expectation that it will be possible to amortize jigs, fixtures, patterns, and any other costs over the length of the job. The company has refused to manufacture one new machine, in which there are many bought-in parts, unless it sees a good chance of producing not less than (say) 200 in a year. This calculation does not make it possible to deduce the required minimum yield on investment. The company, however, feels certain that business on this scale would be worth while. There is little doubt, that, given the decision to stay in business, it is.

(c) FIRM OF MEDIUM GROWTH-RATE IN ENGINEERING

This company, of medium size, makes specialized equipment and devises processes for a range of industries which show, on the whole, a medium rate of growth. Five per cent of its employees are engaged on research and development work, and the expenditure involved is $1\frac{1}{2}$ per cent of turnover.

From 1948 to 1955 the value of output increased $2\frac{1}{2}$ times. To finance this growth the firm became a public company, and it has raised new capital by the sale of shares on four occasions. During this period the finance of expansion was simple compared with the difficulty of changing the organization from a personal to a functional basis.

Since the War both the volume and the range of production have been greatly expanded. The most important cause of this is that during the War the company grew to meet war-time demands. After the War it decided to find uses for its enlarged productive capacity. This policy decision was influenced by the rise of a new generation to the top level of management. At the time the prospective profits of expansion were thought to be high, and it was quite easy to raise new capital. There was an intense demand for the specialized products of the company, for the industries served were expanding output or starting to make more and more use of modern ideas. However, the long-term demand for these specialized products did not seem so certain, and there was a desire to diversify and to spread risk. As the company developed its range of output it moved into more competitive fields, and this has given a strong incentive to create ways of constantly improving products and processes of manufacture.

The expenditure on reasearch and development (at $1\frac{1}{2}$ per cent of turnover) is thought by the company to be at the optimum. A greater expenditure would lead to more potential development than the company could assimilate. There is no research of a long-term nature. Projects are short-term because of the almost non-stop sales pressure for items wanted at once.

The firm takes trouble to collect ideas for new *products* (which may be new *processes* for another industry) as well as for its own methods of production. In addition to its research and development department, the sales department (of chemists and engineers) is 'abnormally research-minded' and productive of ideas.

When the company was smaller and more specialized many possible new projects were certainly investigated and evaluated, but this process was technical rather than financial, and there was little attempt to estimate probable yields on capital invested. The company's prosperity was based on the intelligent use of a group of patents and associated 'know-how'. Now that the company is public, the output more diverse, and the level of capital expenditure very much greater, the company is endeavouring to institute a much more definite and efficient process of financial evaluation, which entails an accurate estimate of the capital expenditure, a forecast of revenues and costs, and consideration of the effect of potential projects on the balance of the business and its profits.

Most ideas for new projects require research or development work or both. There may be a preliminary and informal consideration of an idea in very broad terms by the sales and technical directors. If thought worthy of further attention the project goes to the research and development committee, which is composed of the scientific manager, chief engineer, chief designer, laboratory manager, and those in charge of research work in the company's main fields of interest. This commitee sends new ideas forward for more detailed examination, or rejects them. In most cases the sales picture is 'pretty clear cut', but where there is doubt sales surveys are made. With a brand-new product it is impossible to make a market survey —only a guess can be made at the potential market and the company's likely share of it.

Items agreed upon at this committee come under a system of 'development numbers' by which development expenditure is authorized; any major expenditure has to be passed in this way—if it were very large, the approval of the Board might have to be sought. The Board is often involved at various stages before a final decision is taken. There is no general rule as to whether financial calculations will figure in the investigation from the word 'go', or whether they will come in at a much later stage. Sometimes it is not possible to do costing until the prototype is being designed, for it is only gradually as the product is developed that all the factors involved can be seen. By then the matter may have to be considered less favourably than at the beginning.

When a piece of research and development work is complete, and this includes the making of prototypes and sometimes pre-production runs, the results are placed before the appropriate technical committee. The technical evaluation, together with capital-equipment requirements and the estimates of financial implications, then go to the managing director, who takes a decision on the advice of the sales, production, and technical directors, unless the proposition is of such magnitude that the decision must be made by the Board.

The advice of the sales department, based on market surveys of one kind or another (usually fairly simple) plays an important part at all stages in the choice of projects for research and development and in the decisions about capital expenditure on innovations. The 'pressure for innovation' from the sales department is strong. Indeed, it is felt that it is too strong on certain occasions; the company feels that most of the projects which have not turned out successfully since the War have failed because sales pressure has induced them to undertake 'premature development'.

For the past four to five years the company has prepared annual sales surveys. These are arrived at on the basis of general intelligence and on a knowledge of 'what is cooking'. The precision which can be attached to them varies a great deal. In certain cases it is quite clear that there is a big opportunity and that the market is virtually assured; in others there is no such certainty, while if a brand-new product is being considered all that can be done is to guess at the potential market and the company's share of it. Taken together, forecasts have been very nearly right, although there have been gross errors in particular lines.

The investigation of technical and sales possibilities and their relation to the company's overall financial position, both at an intermediate stage and when the final decision is taken, eliminates a good deal of the uncertainty involved in investment decisions. The forecasts by the sales department are based on the assumption that present and recent conditions yield 'trends' which may continue. A sales assessment at any given moment will be based on the reasoning that if something in the company's range is markedly better than existing products on the market it will sell.

No minimum return on capital investment is laid down as a criterion for investment decisions. In product innovations the company is not generally interested in anything which would not promise a gross profit of £5,000, e.g. a 25 per cent return for a £20,000 fixed investment. It is considered necessary to have this sort of return to pay off a normal amount of research and development (bearing in mind the unsuccessful development items) and the cost of getting the product into production. There are, however, qualifications to this rule—the company has been willing to accept a smaller return in order to compete with a rival. Also, a project with a longer pay-off period might be preferred to one with a shorter pay-off period if the latter involved new factory space and the former did not. This is particularly so at the moment, when the company has just had to carry out an extensive building programme. The locking up of working capital is taken into account, so that the '25 per cent gross return' may be significantly higher or lower in the final calculation.

In the past it has been non-financial considerations rather than financial ones which have been most important in reaching the decsion to undertake investment, though there is no precise information on their nature. During the post-war years the company had several capital issues, and in arranging these the amount of money necessary for new projects known to be coming up was borne in mind. The nature of taxation and the amount left after its payment have not prevented the taking up of research and development projects, but where profit margins have fallen this has led to delay in modernization of equipment. Recently a considerable squeezing of profit margins has slowed down capital expenditure. Projects are now perforce tailored to funds available, and this has altered the ranking of investment projects; it has also further altered the choice of development projects, but the company is not yet adapted to its new situation of greater size and greater competition, nor is it adapted to the need for more long-term planning to avoid financial stringency.

(d) FIRM OF RAPID GROWTH-RATE IN THE MODERN SECTOR

This is a small and young company. It employs 12 per cent of its employees on research and development, it is in a highly competitive field, and it serves with intermediate products a number of expanding industries. In most cases it is providing a new material to do a job hitherto done by traditional materials. Output has grown rapidly since 1943.

The firm grew from the consultancy work of an engineer who was dissatisfied with the materials then available. He started a company to sell a new material which he developed. From subsequent research work new products and uses were developed and sales grew rapidly. Starting from a vision that the industry must grow rapidly to fully automatic production methods, there has been a constant drive to reduce the numbers employed on existing processes by the provision of automatic equipment. There has also been the desire to grow both along existing lines, and by the introduction of new products. The key members of the firm still have painful memories of the five years before they managed to break even, and of the difficulty of expansion because of lack of capital and goodwill for their new firm.

The opportunity for productive investment has come from both inside and outside the company. There has been an increasing demand for the company's products, and successful research and development work has provided a growing number of new processes and products. However, there has been considerable difficulty in raising the necessary capital, working as well as fixed. After a severe early struggle to survive, the firm ploughed back all its profits after taxation and expanded with the assistance of bank loans. However, lack of finance was a considerable impediment to expansion. The company was too new and small for a public issue, and the very firm ideas of the founder about the direction and proper objectives of the company prevented its absorption by interested public companies in Britain. This problem was partly solved by sale to a foreign firm with whom the company already had contact on technical matters and which found it satisfactory to leave control with the founder. The parent firm financed a large increase in fixed investment. Nevertheless, there are self-imposed limits on expansion due to a desire of the company not to call on the parent firm for additional working capital.

The results of research and development activities provide much of the data on which decisions to invest are taken. The research department is efficient in its choice of problems, its collection and sifting of scientific and technical information, and its use of consultants and contacts. As is to be expected in an efficient small firm which lacks financial reserves and is building up markets, research is short term rather than long term. There is a close integration between development, production, and sales departments. Thus when a member of the research department is assigned responsibility for a project he not only takes it through the development stage but is also responsible for the initial sales and 'trouble shooting'. Only then is the new item handed over to the production department. Research staff are thus both 'production' and 'sales-minded'. Such an arrangement gives the impression that the risks are taken in the research and development stage. This is not quite true, however, for productive investment is often approved before the project is fully proven. The dominance of the research and development department sometimes gives the impression that the decision is based on technical rather than on financial considerations. It must be remembered that the company is so small that there are frequent discussions between directors, departmental heads, and project leaders. Apart from major projects, such as new factories, decisions are mainly taken by the management committee composed of the managing director, sales director, research manager, works manager, and secretary.

The sense of financial pressure is strong. Because of this, financial considerations are always taken into account in choosing between technical projects. The company works to an annual budget which is based on an estimate of sales turnover for the coming year. It has earned a high reputation for the technical service it provides and, since a feature of its selling is 'customer-education', an intimate knowledge of markets is developed. The fact that the company has a comparatively large sales force—about 15 per cent of total personnel —enables well-informed views on market trends to be available.

The company carefully weighs up projects from the point of view of capital available and capital needed for expansion. For a large project, such as a new factory, additional money is sought from banks or from the 'parent' company. For other expenditure the company relies on its own resources, and works within an annual budget based on an estimate of sales turnover in the coming year. In consequence, there is a strong bias towards projects that pay for themselves quickly and expenditure on equipment is sensitive to current levels of available profits. The fact that the company does not have a minimum-yield basis of deciding the worthwhileness of investment projects is not at all surprising. Because it is small and has a close link between the technical and financial forms of appraisal, it can make an apparently general form of choice between investment projects. Given the preliminary appraisal, it is fairly easy to decide which project or projects are best suited to the market position and the financial resources of the firm.

(e) FIRM OF MEDIUM GROWTH-RATE IN THE MODERN SECTOR

The company is in a section of industry in which the provision for research in universities and research institutes is good, and the rate of introduction of new products, most of which are branded, is high. It employs 1,500 people. Between 1948 and 1956 net tangible assets grew by just less than 100 per cent, and the value of sales increased almost as much. Trading profit increased 150 per cent, with a random high point in 1951 and a low point in 1952. One-half of this expansion was financed internally; for the other half there was a fairly even distribution between equity and loan capital.

The motives for investment are varied but clear. The rate of change in product and process in the industry is high. The firm has a general interest in innovation as a condition for survival, and a particular interest in development in its own special field. The demand for the products of the industry is an increasing function of population, of the standard of living, and of research activity. The expected increase in all three gives a confidence in an upward trend of the market, and therefore in the continuing opportunity for profitable investment. Other motives for investment in innovation are the desire for prestige (both in itself and as a financial asset), and the observed effect of expansion on the morale of executives and workers.

The company does not undertake long-term research. Its new products result from market evaluation of, and production-development work on, known scientific or process developments in the industry. Those doing research are part of the staff of different production units, and their time is divided (in varying proportions) between research, development, and production. A fair estimate of the number involved in research is 2 per cent of those employed.

Ideas for possible new products come from a variety of sources— from published research (particularly that occurring in fields where the company is already active), from the sales department, from the company's technical information department, or from a feeling that there might be a useful new product to be obtained from an existing by-product. Such ideas are considered at regular meetings of Board members, comprising the chairman and the heads of the operating divisions. Here they confine attention to the choice of projects for research and development, and at this stage, investigation and evaluation is almost wholly commercial rather than technical.

The company distinguishes two types of project:

(*a*) Where the arguments for or against the project are thought to be so clear-cut that it is unnecessary for the company to go into great detail.

(*b*) Where there is a need to be selective. Since the War there have always been more attractive propositions open to the company than it can undertake. The weighing-up of one against the other takes account of—

(i) the probable length of life of the product or process;

(ii) the likely level of sales in home and overseas markets;

(iii) the nature of the requirements of scientific and other trained staff, and the relation of this to the training and experience of existing staff;

(iv) the raw material supplies;

(v) the building and space required, and (since rapidity of development is very important) whether or not they are *readily* available.

Based on this information—part of which is factual and part of which involves personal judgements—an estimate is made, for the potential investment, of the expected total earnings on capital (fixed and working). A provisional investment decision is made at this stage.

Where the subsequent technical investigation proves to be in rough accordance with the expectation of the directors concerned, the decision taken at the earlier meeting of directors quickly becomes a decision to invest in productive resources, unless there has been a significant change in the market trends in the meantime.

Because of the high rate of change, forecasting is very difficult. Judgement about the 'probable length of life of the product' is sometimes very uncertain. Where no one really knows if another product can be produced to supersede it, the advice of a specialist within the firm (often a member of the Board) is sought, so that (it is said) 'judgement can be made on a fair amount of fact'. The assessment of potential markets, in order to judge the required scale of production, is based on general factors, such as intelligence gathered by the sales staff, 'knowledge of what is going on in the trade', and an unsophisticated extension and use of relevant Government statistics. In the export field a certain amount of factual data is available, and this is used, together with an assessment of individual markets by men on the spot.

The company is conscious of but not tortured by the uncertain nature of its forecasts. Later technical development and evaluation remove one part of the uncertainty. For the rest the best thing to do is to get as much factual information as possible and on this basis to make a judgement. The various directors—specialists in their own sphere—contribute to the judgement, and it is felt that in this way the group makes reasonable decisions, because they are based on all existing information.

The company must take risks, and where there is doubt about the forecast, then the potential yield on capital is 'put sufficiently high to counteract the risk'. There is, however, no evidence of a scale of measurement for risk. The informal nature of the decision-taking, which places a stress on oral communication of judgements and forecasts on this and that, probably leads to a varying reaction to risk. Furthermore, a reaction to risk that varies with the financial position of the company is, in these conditions, to be expected. Thus the sharp fall of profits and sales in 1952 reduced the capacity of the company to undertake risky projects at that time, even if it left the basic attitude to taking risks unaffected. The willingness to take a risk is also affected by such things as the need to introduce new skills. Where a risky project entails the recruitment of new forms of skill the sense of risk is increased, because there has been an increase in the number of explicit unknowns.

The decision to proceed with investment in a new product or process is based on the criterion that the capital investment—fixed and working—is expected to yield at least a certain amount. But the amount so fixed varies between 10 and 30 per cent. The nature of this reckoning reveals that risk is doubly discounted. For, on the one hand, if the project is regarded as risky a higher prospective yield is required for action, and on the other hand, in the calculations for a risky project the equipment is written off quickly. As a consequence, the firm rarely makes a tremendous profit from the introduction of an outstanding new product or runs the risk of a big loss from an innovation.

Another important factor is the absolute size of the investment involved. A new product requiring, say, less than $\frac{1}{2}$ per cent of the net assets of the company would not be worth 'the time and effort required to talk about it', even if the prospective yield was very high. On the other hand, annual investments above a certain sum, say 10 per cent of assets, are treated as beyond the capacity of the company.

The limit set by 'what the company knows it can do' is not simply a matter of capacity to find finance. It is also affected by the firm's conception of capacity to manage. This is determined in a rather vague way by the concept of a manageable number of new developments each year, and by the sense of what can be achieved with existing staff in the higher levels of management.

Replacement, by similar or improved plant, and the purchase of additional plant of small magnitude, are, within the limits of annual depreciation charges, in large measure regarded as a matter of 'staying in business'. Directors of operating departments are asked not to approve capital expenditure in any one year in excess of the depreciation allowance for that year. Such decisions are not reduced to a 'potential yield' basis unless the expenditure is autonomous—i.e. induced neither by the wearing out of existing equipment, nor by the demand for increased output, nor by the competitive need to improve quality.

Where a higher level of capital expenditure is required by operating departments for replacements which embody improvements, the procedure is nearer that described for new products—except where the continuance of the firm in its main lines of activity is in question, when the decision may fall into the category of 'those where the advantages are self-evident'.

(f) FIRM OF RAPID GROWTH IN THE MODERN SECTOR

This is a large (but not a very large) company in a 'modern' industry. The ratio of capital to labour is high, and 5 per cent of those employed are engaged in research and development. Between 1948 and 1955 the value of sales increased over four-fold, and net tangible assets and trading profits increased three-fold. In the same period the capital/labour ratio increased 70 per cent. The finance of this expansion was 40 per cent internal, 40 per cent by sale of shares, and 20 per cent by debentures. The profits and prospects were so good that there was no difficulty about frequent and large issues of new capital.

The motives for investment—in this case for a high rate of investment—are three. First, the industry is dynamic and competitive. Innovation in product and process is assumed to be a condition of survival. Second, given the level of research and development in the industry, and the expanding markets, the opportunities for profitable investment in innovation are many. Third, with 5 per cent employed (and these mostly 'staff') on research and development the internal pressure to use opportunities for innovation is considerable.

Investment projects are of two kinds: 'manufacturing' (the installation of plant to make something to sell) and 'non-manufacturing' (service projects, such as a new canteen or research building). The first type of project sets the investment programme, and the second is 'tied in' to service it at the minimum cost. Ideas for new projects can come from a variety of sources—from the research department, from sales reports that the market for a particular product is growing, or from a desire to make an intermediate product which the company is at present buying.

Irrespective of its source, the development department will initiate the project. This company has evolved a definite pattern of investigation and evaluation for projects at various stages in their development. One individual from the development department is charged with steering the idea through the various stages, decisions are taken successively by persons or bodies with increasing authority, and at ecah stage the project is handled by persons specializing in that stage.

In the initial stages the development department prepares a rough outline of the project in terms of the raw-material position, the production and engineering feasibility, the volume of sales, and the capital requirements. In the first stages of a project, market estimates are rough approximations (very rough for a *new* product) based on, for example, knowledge of the United States market and a guess at the volume of demand and of potential competition. If early investigation indicates the wisdom of proceeding, market research is undertaken and more detailed estimates are prepared. It will then be possible to prepare a slightly more accurate report on what the project may involve. When the project has been clearly defined the engineering department makes rough input–output estimates, after which the estimating department makes a more refined estimate. After further work and consideration it is possible for the engineering department to make a pretty accurate estimate of production costs. At the same time estimates are also made by sales staff. This information then goes to the development committee, which sifts and ranks the projects. The development committee is made up of representatives of sales, production, engineering, research, and development departments. If the project is approved, the mechanical design department will prepare an estimate from tender figures and a revised production-cost estimate will be produced which, along with sales estimates, will come into the capital budget.

Forecasts are made with varying degrees of accuracy at the different stages of investigation. In the first stages of appraising a proposed new product they are rough approximations, but later market research is undertaken to make possible the preparation of detailed estimates. In estimating the future market the company is greatly guided by United States trends. It is assumed that United States growth factors will operate here with a time lag.

In forecasting it is assumed that, by and large, selling prices move with costs. Current materials costs and selling prices are used for estimates unless it is 'known' that costs are going to move abnormally with reference to other things. Thus, in recent years, it has been assumed that the cost of plant would rise 5–7 per cent per annum. Where a new product is involved it is assumed in estimating that, due to competition, the future price will fall relative to costs. Depreciation charges are based on Inland Revenue conventions.

The critical forecast is that of the future state of the market. If growth has been steady, and if comparison with the earlier trend in the United States indicates that it should continue, the forecast is made with confidence and is insensitive to short-term fluctuations.

The company has many worth-while projects and (on the ground that it earns more in plant) it dislikes idle money. If, therefore, current sales fall significantly below expectation the capital budget will be affected. In the 1952 recession, items had to be taken off the capital budget because of the shortage of funds for capital expenditure. The revision of the capital budget, however, was not simply a matter of eliminating the requisite number of lowest-yield projects—

there was also a revision of growth expectation on the part of the
sales staff. Such a revision was not made for all commodities, but
only for the commodities, about which there was least information.
Where, as in the case of products linked to the demand for rubber,
there was thought to be sufficient information to establish the long-
term growth factor, the slump in current sales was ignored.

The company's view is that there are so many possible projects
that there is not much point in spending time on being uncertain.
Where the estimators do feel a substantial uncertainty the project
will in fact not rank high in the 'prospective-yield' list. Great care is
taken to reduce uncertainty. Thus projects will not reach the stage
of submission to the Board until, in the manner described above, the
research, development, and sales departments have made substantial investigations into techniques, costs, and market potential.

Some uncertainties may take a long time to resolve. Thus, a raw
material may be difficult to get, and there may be long and tedious
negotiations with the supplier on both price and output; or there
may be protracted negotiations with a principal customer. Here no
action is taken until the uncertainty is resolved. The yield prospect
affects the energy with which the negotiations are carried through.

The company policy is to put in plant of such a size that it will be
able to work to capacity in one or two years. Estimates of profit are
based on the assumption that equipment will work to 80 per cent of
capacity. But estimates are also made of costs at 100, 70, and 50 per
cent of the probable rate of plant capacity. Where costs rise steeply
with a fall in use of capacity, the project will rank low unless the
market forecast is such that output at at least 80 per cent of capacity
is thought certain. Where there is a conflict in estimating market
potential the sales department estimate is used. Uncertainty is also
catered for by the convention that with a new product a higher
minimum yield is required than for an established product.

In general, the decision to proceed with investment in a new project is based on a forecast that the capital invested will yield a minimum of 20 per cent *before* tax (interest not being included as a cost).
There are, however, qualifications to this generalization. If the product being considered is a new one, then the company would expect
a higher rate of return than on some basic commodity; if there is a
low raw-material cost and high conversion cost the company would
proceed only if there was promise of a big volume of output; if there
is a high break-even point the project must be very sound from the
sales point of view. A plant with a low yield might be put in if it was

felt that otherwise the company would lose a market for a standard product. That is, the company would in such a case be taking into account not only the yield on the plant but also the effect on the present profit of a greater strength of competition. For a new process, however, direct money yield is the sole motive power.

The Board may reject a big project put forward by the development committee on grounds of policy or because of a different judgement of the market and the competitive position. There may be a decision to drop a project because it would involve direct competition with X, who is very strong, or with Y, who is an important customer.

The question of timing depends on the development of the market, and this in turn is related to the company's views about the absolute size of the operation in which it is interested. The project may be judged to be 'not big enough at present', and it may be decided, on the basis of present growth rates, to look again at the matter in a certain number of years.

There is no difficulty in raising money in this industry, other than the usual Capital Issues Committee directives. A rise in the rate of interest *might* eliminate a few marginal projects; interest is not included as a cost, but an increase in the rate of interest might push up the minimum yield expected.

Nine Summary and implications

It is not easy to reduce the vast disorder of facts about investment in innovation to an odrerly scheme; and indeed it is dangerous to begin with an intention of discovering an orderliness which may not exist. There may, of course, be, despite the various nature and habits of different firms, a statistical orderliness about their actions when large numbers are taken together. Evidence of such statistical regularity is contained in a recent study of the actions of firms in the United States;[1] this suggests that in the short run investment is strongly influenced by liquidity (that is to say, by the cash surplus becoming available as a difference between the profits from current operations and an established or conventional dividend): while in the long run the custom of producers is to maintain a relatively fixed relationship between capital and output. The data for British 'quoted' public companies, collected for the period since 1949 by the National Institute for Economic and Social Research and the Board of Trade, might (with some collection of additional facts) serve as foundation for a similar study for the United Kingdom, and we hope that such a study will be undertaken. Nevertheless, we should be disposed to be extremely cautious in the use of conclusions based on broad aggregates measured over short periods of years; the conditions of the period 1949–57, for instance, were strongly influenced by Government policies and by external events which will never be repeated in the same pattern again.

We consider, in fact, that any use of the aggregative and statistical approach must be supported by an understanding of the actions of business men. Business men are, after all, human beings with minds and wills of their own, with their own preferences and oddities, with their own ways of influencing each other; they are not, like the molecules of a gas, similar objects dancing about and colliding in a random manner. Like the hoops, balls, and mallets in Alice's game of croquet, they have a tendency to upset the laws of the game by

[1] J. R. Meyer and E. Kuh, *The Investment Decision*, Cambridge, Mass., Harvard University Press, 1957.

manifesting an ability for independent movement. We have tried in this book to make a small contribution to the study of the complexity of business behaviour. Our data, and therefore out interests, have been mainly directed to investment in new technical and scientific ideas—an important element in capital expenditure, present to some degree in a great part of fixed investment, but nevertheless much less than the whole of industry's investment operations. We would not expect to find (and have not in fact found) in this limited field evidence of a close relation to liquidity, this being a factor whose effects would be seen in the total of investment, including that in stocks of goods and work in progress; nor have we found evidence of fixed capital–output ratios, which would be discovered (if they exist) by a study of the extension of capital, and not of its transformation by new knowledge.

We have given more space to the desire to invest than to the ability to find the funds to do so. This does not mean that we have failed to recognize the importance of financial limitations. In the earlier stages of our investigations it was a minority (though an important and progressive minority) of the firms we visited who appeared to find the difficulty of raising or retaining money a serious hindrance; in the later stages monetary stringency was increasing, but it still remained true that a goodly proportion of firms were in a state of comfortable liquidity. There is in any case no doubt that the Government and the Bank of England are able, by fiscal and monetary measures, to modify the ease with which companies retain or raise money; to discover a truth so obvious would not be very helpful. The interesting variations are in the desire of companies to invest, and the question we have had in mind is 'What are the conditions which would strengthen the willingness to invest in innovation?' In discussing this we shall, however, say a little about the influence of the price of money, that is of the complex of rates of interest on new borrowings.

The elements of a decision to invest in innovation are a technical opportunity, a stimulus to action, and a means of deciding the best form of action. In Chapter Two we suggested that 'the nursery-grounds where we must look for technical opportunities of investment, well grown and ready for planting out' are the research and development (or design) departments of the firm concerned, or the sales departments of supply firms, or some other body which carries through the development of a discovery to the point of commercial exploitation. The origin of the idea may have been far back, perhaps in the genius of some inventive individual; but it has no significance for investment until it has passed, in some firm or institution, through the difficult and costly stage of development or design. If there is to be a flow of adopted innovations, there must be a flow of original ideas; this is in part a matter of chance, but is in part determined by the quality and nature of the educational system, and by the extent of the nation's investment in pure and applied research. In addition, there must be an effective choice of ideas for the stage of development, and an adequate investment of resources in development.

It is therefore highly significant that there has been a recent and rapid rise in British expenditure on industrial research and development. Such expenditure has its full effect on the flow of investment opportunities only after a considerable lapse of time. In the early stages of research and development the staff tends to be used on long-term or basic research, or on 'trouble-shooting'—that is, on dealing with difficulties occurring in current production. Where scientists have not previously been employed there are usually many of these difficulties awaiting their attention. Where (as in many traditional industries) there was little scientific knowledge of the nature of the materials and processes, basic research is often a prerequisite of practical development. Thus it is only after a period that a true research and development programme, yielding a flow of technical opportunities for investment, can come into being.

Thus the flow of investment opportunities is likely to show an accelerated rise in the future. Since we believe that the decision to commit resources to research, design and development is 'the prime mover in the creation of investment opportunities' (this creation of opportunities being by no means confined to the firms undertaking the research) it follows that the technical opportunities to invest will tend to be increased by any of the following:

1 A more adequate number of people, willing to devote their energies to the work of industry, who are scientifically literate.

2 Better communication of ideas.

3 A larger investment in pure or applied research.

4 A larger investment in development and design, including the construction of prototypes and pilot plants.

5 More effective direction of research and development, including a better choice of projects and a lessening of waste effort.

Behind these stand in turn such issues as the extent of State aid for research, and the total flow of scientifically trained staff capable of undertaking research and development or of appreciating its results.

In Chapter Four we have examined at some length the complexities contained in the idea that the stimulus to action, to take advantage of a technical opportunity to invest, is expected money profit. This examination is far from showing that profit is unimportant—indeed, in the larger firms it may be the most obvious stimulus to action, and in no firm can the long-run need to make profit be ignored. But we do suggest that the definition and method of use of the 'profit criterion' will vary greatly from firm to firm, so that no tidy consistency of response can be expected. Furthermore, other factors—prestige, technical pride, susceptibility to sales pressure, the desire to copy competitors, the need to replace out-of-date plant or to shorten an excessive order book—must be listed as possible stimuli, additional or alternative to the maximization of profit. The conjunction of an idea with a man with the drive to have it carried out is important. Further, a stimulus sufficient to produce prompt action in one firm may fail to penetrate the elephantine hide of another. Therefore some attention must be given to parochialism, to the barriers of ignorance and apathy by which some firms protect themselves from the inconvenient incursion of new ideas. Investment in innovation is likely to be greater and more timely if firms are able to attract to their management and to their technical posts lively minds, keen to reach out and pull in new ideas, and not satisfied with the automatic repetition of past procedures. The lack of men of sufficient ability for senior management is an important reason for caution in using technical advance.

Our discussion in Chapter Seven of methods of prediction shows, among other things, that the stimulus to action frequently comes from an inescapable need to replace worn-out plant, or from immediate excess demand, or from a strong long-run expectation of rising demand. Elsewhere we refer to the importance of the interrelations of firms—to the stimulating influence of suppliers of materials or machinery, or of customers who are particular about their requirements. This 'chain effect' is of the utmost importance; it means that the extent of investment in innovation is related not only to certain conditions which create opportunities (such as 1 to 5 above) but also to the effectiveness with which the stimulus from these opportunities can be communicated from firm to firm. Thus it is important that scientifically literate people should be well spread over industry, in order that such communication may be swift and effective along an unbroken chain of receptive firms.

In addition to the general conditions which favour the creation of investment opportunities, there are various conditions which are likely to stimulate firms to accept these opportunities, or which increase their ability to take the chances open to them. These are conditions which favour investment in innovation in *particular firms or industries*, but we would stress that no one condition is general in its effect. For instance, a more generous treatment of industrial profits may have little effect on a parochial firm which is unconscious of technical oportunities, and which lacks the skill to assess their consequences even if it finds out their existence. The list which follows should therefore be regarded as a way of setting out some important influences, not as a set of policy recommendations.

6 A lowering of taxation on industrial profits.
7 Easier terms for obtaining industrial risk capital.

These would increase the ability of some firms (such as company (d) in Chapter Eight) to press forward with investment, and they might also offer a greater incentive to do so.

8 In some industries, keener home or foreign competition.
9 In some industries, greater protection or less competition, so that a longer view may be taken.

This opposed pair gives a reminder that some industries or firms become technically progressive because they are prodded by competition, while others are helped by protection; no general rule applies.[1]

10 Excess demand, or the expectation of high and rising demand in the future.

We have noted the importance of this stimulus on p. 71. The condition carries the awkward implication that inflationary conditions may be good for technical advance; it should therefore be added that excess demand must not be such as to cause a galloping inflation or a serious loss of foreign markets.

11 The improvement of recruitment and training for management and for technical and scientific posts.

[1] See *Industry and Technical Progress*, pp. 163–9.

Condition 1 above relates to the existence of scientifically literate people; condition 11 relates to the need for a plan of action to ensure that the firm gets and trains its fair share of talent.

12 Quicker obsolescence (that is, a readiness to scrap plant and machinery earlier).

This might be encouraged by changes in the tax system, but it is largely a matter of the conventions and habits of industry.

13 Measures which by propaganda or example increase the receptiveness of parochial firms.

Because there are many kinds of stimuli, there are many methods of selecting the best forms of action. Those firms which think first of the maximization of profit sometimes use elaborate methods of producing money estimates, though some go no farther than rough estimates of an expected pay-off period. We have at a number of points, however, drawn attention to the foolishness of taking apparently exact money estimates as being just what they seem. Some have built into them the pessimism and caution of successive estimators, and their apparent precision conceals the fact that large contingency allowances have been included; others express a mood of optimism, and are liable to abrupt change if conditions alter for the worse. The differences between the estimates of yield and the actual yields are considerable, and this shows that it is proper to lay much stress on the uncertainties of the future, many of which are irreducible even to the most careful and forward-looking firm. Yet we find that in the particular circumstances of the mid-1950's grave uncertainty did not affect many of the investment decisions we studied; and this reflects the fact that many decisions were due to the stimulus of immediate excess demand, an immediate need for replacement, or a strong expectation of early increases of demand, so that they fell into the class of decisions for which the reasons are 'obvious' and money estimates are hardly thought necessary. Because of this, and also because many firms lack the statistical and accounting ability required for the making of good money estimates, we found that most of the investment decisions studied were taken without explicit consideration of yield.

Where expected yields were calculated, they varied over a very wide range; high yields were found to be expected in progressive industries (though they were variously defined), and they were associated with a high level of research and development expenditure, with 'long views' in the conduct of research and development, and with *confidence* (rather than uncertainty) in facing the markets of the future. But the fact that much of the investment was felt to be obviously necessary, and that few decisions were taken under a grave sense of uncertainty, must have been favourable to the adoption of innovation. This suggests that innovation is likely to be helped by:

14 The absence of expectations of violent changes of conditions (including sudden and considerable changes of Government policy).

We have suggested that the tendency to vary the conditions under which nationalized industries operate, to fit the short-term variations of national circumstances, is probably harmful to innovation in those industries.

We have found little direct evidence of the regulatory effect of rates of interest. This matter deserves, however, fuller consideration. It is first of all clear that the numerous firms which do not (and perhaps cannot) express their decisions in figures can only be affected by a change of rates of interest through the intermediary of the effect of such change on general business sentiment, or on the expected growth of markets, or on the ease or difficulty of raising money (which is not wholly determined by its price). Likewise those decisions which, though they take place in firms which sometimes make estimates of yield, were not in fact quantified, are only subject to these indirect influences. The indirect influences may be considerable—we would certainly not wish to underestimate the importance of general business sentiment—but they are not automatic. Second, where explicit estimates of yield are made they are frequently as high as 20 per cent, and a change of 1 or 2 per cent in rates of interest may in effect already be adequately discounted in the contingency allowances buried in the estimate of yield. The change in rates during the main period of our case-studies was not in fact very great.

We have, however, identified a few decisions where a yield, estimated without undue pessimism, would, after payment of tax, pay no more than the currently expected return on capital, and where it seemed likely that an increase in rates of interest might cause the decisions to be altered.[1] In other words, there *are* investment deci-

[1] We should no doubt have found many such decisions if we had examined investment in housing.

sions which are 'marginal' in relation to rates of interest; and it seems to us possible that under other circumstances the marginal class might be greatly increased. First, it was suggested to us that the apparent irrelevance of rate of interest changes was due to the fact that the United Kingdom had never experienced really high rates; that a small change in a rate around 5 per cent may be of little significance to projects whose gross yield before tax is expected to be 20 per cent, but that a small change in a rate around 8 or 9 per cent would be of vital importance. We think that it is certainly true that the marginal class would be much more important at higher rates. Second, an easing of excess demand and a period of uncertainty in the trend of demand (such as has in fact occurred in 1958) would reduce the relative importance of non-quantified decisions, and increase the relative importance of decisions sensitive to the rate of interest. In other words, the control exercised by high rates of interest begins to 'bite' only *after* the excess demand has been eliminated, and the rising trend of demand interrupted or rendered uncertain. Putting the matter more generally, where business expectations are firm and decisions are easily arrived at—either to expand, when demand is high, or to do nothing, when there is a slump—rates of interest would have little controlling effect; at the intermediate stages of doubt and uncertainty their effect, though far from universal, might be much more significant.

We must emphasize that these are views founded on our classification of investment decisions, but not on direct observation. The high rates of interest prevalent at the time at which we *wrote* this book were accompanied by a certain amount of rationing of credit, and it would not have been easy to sort out the effects of the high cost of raising money from those of the difficulty of raising it at any price.

We have given above fourteen conditions which may be expected to encourage investment in innovation. The problem as it presents itself to the Government, however, is a double one: both to keep investment (and especially innovatory investment) at a high level, and to keep the total of investment at a level which can be supported without excessive inflation. This level of investment depends on such things as the total of production within the country, the net income from abroad, the desired or permitted level of consumption, and the size of Government current expenditure on goods and services; it is subject to fluctuation, and we have considered whether our studies (though confined to investment in innovation) throw any light on the means of controlling this fluctuation.

The long-term aim of keeping innovatory investment at a high level—that is, of speeding up technical progress—is harmed by sudden changes; and this suggests that it is very desirable that the changes which the Government considers it necessary to make should be in consumption rather than in investment. The analysis of Chapter Seven suggests that some investment will be sensitive to two interrelated influences which are capable of short-run change, namely the extent of excess demand and the size of profits. But the change is not necessarily very rapid; an order book many months long may have to shorten a lot before investment plans are changed; an empty order book may have to fill up considerably before new investment is undertaken. Profits are dependent on many factors special to particular industries, and their size is difficult to control. In order to make any regulation of investment effective more quickly, a Government would have to create not only an immediate change but a change in expectations for the future; that is to say, it would have to bring home to industry the idea that demand or profits were not only falling (or rising) but must be expected to go on falling (or rising). The creation of such changes of business sentiment is doubtless possible, in favourable circumstances, but it is not automatic; nor would it necessarily be desirable for the Treasury to become skilled in these arts of psychological warfare.

We do not therefore rate highly the chances of controlling the volume of fixed investment (whether in private or in nationalized industry) to fit the short-term changes of economic circumstances, except by means which will harm the long-run aim of achieving rapid technical advance. It may be that control can be achieved through variations of social investment, or 'public works', of a kind whose economic function is slight or indirect. But after examining the complexity of the actions of firms, we are not surprised that investment in the 1950's has taken a course which has at times been an embarrassment to Government planners.

Appendix Traditional ideas of the decision process

Our argument in this book has distinguished between the technical opportunities of investment and the reactions of business men to these opportunities. This is not a distinction which appears frequently or clearly in economic literature. In general, the opportunities for investment have been taken for granted, or assumed to be something given by chance or by causes external to the economic system, or mysteriously created by the beneficent interplay of competition. The idea of innovation as being a professional activity is, however, firmly stated by Adam Smith. After writing of inventions made by workmen, he goes on:

Many improvements have been made by the ingenuity of the makers of the machines, when to make them became the business of a peculiar trade; and some by that of those who are called philosophers, or men of speculation, whose trade it is not to do any thing, but to observe every thing, and who, upon that account, are often capable of combining together the powers of the most distant and dissimilar objects. In the progress of society, philosophy or speculation becomes, like every other employment, the principal or sole trade and occupation of a particular class of citizens. . . .[1]

Adam Smith's theory is that innovation is the product of the division of labour; that this division depends on the extent of the market, and therefore appears first where markets are enlarged by water-carriage; that the division of labour brings with it opulence and progress, and with this progress the inventor or innovator himself becomes more specialized, and 'the quantity of science is considerably increased'.

This view may be contrasted with those summarized by Haberler, in his comprehensive survey of trade-cycle theory.[2] 'Invention' is here mentioned many times, but most often as a disturbance from outside, to be grouped with wars, crop changes caused by the weather,

---

[1] *Wealth of Nations*, Book I, Chapter I.
[2] *Prosperity and Depression,* 3rd edition, United Nations, 1946.

and spontaneous changes in consumer tastes. Hicks writes[1] of the probable irregularity of innovation, though he considers that innovations may be made more easily or applied more quickly in boom conditions, and that in a slump there may be a shortage of investment opportunities; the creation of these opportunities is to him an activity which is at least on the fringe of the economic system.

To find a modern statement of innovation as a professional activity *within* the economic system, we must turn to Schumpeter. He writes of the social function of entrepreneurs, 'to reform or revolutionize the pattern of production', as losing importance; personality and will power count for less; capitalist enterprise tends to 'automatize progress', and thus to make itself superfluous.

> Innovation itself is being reduced to routine. Technological progress is increasingly becoming the business of teams of trained specialists who turn out what is required and make it work in predictable ways. The romance of earlier commercial adventure is rapidly wearing away, because so many more things can be strictly calculated that had of old to be visualized in a flash of genius.[2]

In writing of the trade of the 'philosopher or speculator' Adam Smith was ahead of his time, for the eighteenth-century inventor was often what would now be called an amateur. But with the growth of research and development as a deliberate industrial activity, a new situation has been created, in which some firms at least are conscious of the relation between what they can invent and what they can invest. Investment becomes in part a planned activity, regulated by a capital budget; innovation is something which must be brought into being, or sought out elsewhere, to provide the opportunities which the capital budget will require. Such ways of thinking are, of course, slow to spread through industry; and they have been slow also to have an effect on professional economists.

Those who have treated innovation as mainly external to the economic system have on occasion supposed also that, with increasing wealth, it would one day be found that no further opportunities of profitable investment remained. The desires of mankind would be satiated; Keynes conceived it possible to bring the 'marginal efficiency'[3] of capital approximately to zero in a single generation.

---

[1] *Value and Capital*, 2nd edition, Oxford University Press, 1946, p. 300.
[2] J. A. Schumpeter, *Capitalism, Socialism and Democracy*, 2nd edition, Allen and Unwin, 1947, p. 132.
[3] See page 113 below.

Hicks, reviewing Keynes' General Theory, pointed out the great importance of such an assumption, though considering it unfortunate that Keynes did not investigate the matter more fully. For the marginal efficiency might be kept up by invention, which would present each generation with new opportunities of investment. 'The whole question of invention thus needs very serious consideration; but I think it will tend to show that a theory which takes into account many dynamic considerations, and then assumes invention nil, should be handled carefully.'[1] A considerable literature has grown up on this issue—for if it could be established that the profitability of capital must fall, rich countries would find it hard to avoid long-term unemployment. Yet the controversy has not led to much attention to the nature of investment opportunities, and to the fundamental point that these are often created by a business decision to devote resources to research and development. There is more to invention than the sudden moment of unexpected inspiration; and, quite contrary to the Keynesian thesis, it is the richest countries which can best create further investment opportunities, because they can afford to devote the resources needed for their creation.

The literature on the reactions of business men to investment opportunities is much more extensive. It shows an interesting progression from vagueness to precision, but the precision is on the whole not an approach to reality; it results from the common habit of removing complications for the sake of clarity in analysis. Unfortunately in this case the complications and the uncertainties are an essential part of the problem.

It is difficult to find in the older economic writings any clear statement of the motives which influence those who engaged in investment in fixed capital. Adam Smith made a distinction between three parts into which the 'general stock' of a country is divided—the stocks of consumer goods, the fixed capital, and the circulating capital. The general line of his discourse, however, fits most closely to the venturing of capital by a merchant in trade, and indeed in his time fixed investment as we now know it was of much slighter importance. To the nineteenth-century economists, the typical manufacturer was one who ventured his own savings, and they regarded the most important decision as being, not the venture of investment, but the prior decision to save. On the one hand, it was assumed that there were investment opportunities waiting for the savings needed

[1] J. R. Hicks, 'Mr. Keynes' Theory of Employment', *Economic Journal*, June 1936, p. 252.

to exploit them; on the other, that savings would emerge in response to the investment opportunities.

It was not assumed that investment would always be profitable. Thus, David Ricardo assumed that (through the operation of forces described in the law of diminishing returns) rising population would put up wages at the expense of profits. This decline of profits would reduce the incentive both to invest and to accumulate savings.

... No one accumulates but with a view to make his accumulation productive.... Without a motive there could be no accumulation.... The farmer and manufacturer can no more live without profit, than the labourer without wages. Their motive for accumulation will diminish with every diminution of profit, and will cease altogether when their profits are so low as not to afford them an adequate compensation for their trouble, and the risk which they must necessarily encounter in employing their capital productively.[1]

In reply to Malthus' contention that if capital accumulation proceeds rapidly prices and profits would fall and cause a deficiency in effective demand, Ricardo allowed that '... the case is possible to conceive of saving being so universal that no profit will arise from the employment of capital', but he asserted that in such a case the capitalist 'without a sufficient motive for saving from revenue, to add to capital, will cease doing so'.[2]

Thus Ricardo believed that savings are made in response to opportunities of profitable investment, and that investment is undertaken in response to the opportunities of increasing profits, being carried to the point where investors are just compensated for their trouble and risk. In this treatment very little is said of the origin and nature of investment opportunities, of the nature of the trouble and risk involved in investing, or of the evidence for the belief that capitalists will in effect maximize the profits to be gained from investment. It is simply assumed that capitalists act rationally and that profit maximization is rational.

John Stuart Mill had more to say about the nature of investment opportunities, though he is vague about the creative process of innovation. On the theory of business decisions he added little to Ricardo's treatment. He speaks in his *Principles of Political Economy*[3] of that 'particular rate of profit, which is the lowest that will induce

[1] *On the Principles of Political Economy and Taxation.* 3rd edition, 1821: Royal Economic Society edition, Cambridge University Press, 1951, vol. I, p. 122.

[2] Royal Economic Society edition of *Works*, Cambridge University Press, 1952, Vol. IX (Letters 1821–3), No. 444.

[3] Book IV, Chapter IV, s. 3.

the people of that country and time to accumulate savings, and to employ those savings productively'. This minimum rate depends on the *time-preference* of the community—that is, on the 'comparative estimate . . . of future interests when weighed against present'—and on the risk involved in employing or lending capital for industrial operations. This risk has a broad dependence on the general security of society, and from the placidity of nineteenth-century optimism Mill writes: 'Destruction by wars, and spoliation by private or public violence, are less and less to be apprehended; and the improvements which may be looked for in education and in the administration of justice, or, in their default, increased regard for opinion, afford a growing protection against fraud and reckless mismanagement.' With this greater security, 'mankind become more willing to sacrifice present indulgence for future objects'; thus both determinants of the minimum rate of profit alter so as to cause the rate to fall, capital expands, and 'would soon reach its ultimate boundary, if the boundary itself did not continually open and leave more space'.[1]

Mill then lists four factors which tend to 'open the boundary' by creating fresh opportunities of investment:[2]

1 'The waste of capital in periods of over-trading and rash speculation, and in the commercial revulsions by which such times are always followed'; but Mill does not follow this up to consider the uncertainties attached to particular investments.

2 Industrial inventions: 'All inventions which cheapen any of the things consumed by the labourers, unless their requirements are raised in an equivalent degree, in time lower money wages: and by doing so, enable a greater capital to be accumulated and employed, before profits fall back to what they were previously.'

3 'The acquisition of any new power of obtaining cheap commodities from foreign countries.'

4 'The perpetual overflow of capital into colonies or foreign countries, to seek higher profits than can be obtained at home'.

It can be seen that these nineteenth-century theories are exceedingly general, relating to the broad tendencies of investment and saving in the whole community. There is no consciousness of any need to discuss the motives of the individual investor. Usually the

[1] *Principles of Political Economy*, Book IV, Chapter IV., s. 4.
[2] Ibid., ss. 5–8.

motives for thrift call for space in the textbooks, rather than the discovery of uses for the money saved.

Marshall, at the end of the century, was too clear-headed to talk of supply without discussing demand, and he at least gives a plain statement of a theory of investment decisions. Supposing the rate of interest to be 4 per cent, he shows how the hat-making trade will push its use of capital until 'the utility of that machinery which it is only just worth their while to employ, is measured by 4 per cent.'[1] In a later chapter he shows how the cost of borrowing money includes, in addition to 'true net interest', allowances for risk of various kinds and perhaps some earnings of management. He therefore allows for the existence of uncertainty on the lender's side but he does not at this point in his argument refer to any difficulty in deciding what the yield of investment may be.

> Each undertaker having regard to his own means, will push the investment of capital in his business in each several direction until what appears in his judgment to be the margin of profitableness is reached; and that margin is, as we have said, a boundary line cutting one after another every possible line of investment, and moving irregularly outwards in all directions whenever there is a fall in the rate of interest at which extra capital can be obtained.[2]

The subjects of risk and uncertainty were extensively treated by F. H. Knight, but his interest is mainly in their effect on profit. 'The prices of the productive services being the costs of production, changes in conditions give rise to profit by upsetting anticipations and producing a divergence between costs and selling price, which would otherwise be equalized by competition.'[3] He writes of investment decisions as 'an exercise of *judgment* of far the highest type called for in the business world',[4] but it cannot be said that he gives a very clear picture of the manner of their taking. In his book *Industrial Fluctuations*, A. C. Pigou shows the great importance of changes in expectations of yield in initiating industrial fluctuations; though he has little to say about the way in which these expectations are formed or about the general influence of uncertainty on the investment process. But he stresses the state of psychological interdependence by which changes of view and errors of forecast spread:

[1] *Principles of Economics* ,Book VI, Chapter I, s. 8.
[2] Ibid.
[3] *Risk, Uncertainty and Profit*, Boston, Houghton Mifflin, 1921, p. 198.
[4] Ibid., p. 325.

A change of tone in one part of the business world diffuses itself, in a quite unreasoning manner, over other and wholly disconnected parts. An expansion of business confidence 'propagates itself by that sympathetic and epidemic excitement which so largely sways communities of men'. There comes into play a quasi-hypnotic system of mutual suggestion:

> One with another, soul with soul,
> They kindle fire from fire. . . .[1]

This is a line of thought which was further developed by Keynes.[2]

To Keynes, in fact, more than to anyone else, we owe the realization of the need for a special study of investment, as being the joint determinant with saving of the level of activity (or of the degree of inflationary pressure) in an economy. Yet it is somewhat disappointing that he did little but add to Marshall's theories a more explicit treatment of the effect of expectations:

When a man buys an investment or capital-asset, he purchases the right to the series of prospective returns, which he expects to obtain from selling its output, after deducting the running expenses of obtaining that output, during the life of the asset. . . . Over against the prospective yield of the investment we have the *supply price* of the capital-asset, meaning by this, not the market-price at which an asset of the type in question can actually be purchased in the market, but the price which would just induce a manufacturer newly to produce an additional unit of such assets, *i.e.* what is sometimes called its *replacement cost*. . . . I define the marginal efficiency of capital as being equal to that rate of discount which would make the present value of the series of annuities given by the returns expected from the capital-asset during its life just equal to its supply price. . . . Now it is obvious that the actual rate of current investment will be pushed to the point where there is no longer any class of capital-asset of which the marginal efficiency exceeds the current rate of interest. In other words, the rate of investment will be pushed to the point on the investment demand-schedule where the marginal efficiency of capital in general is equal to the market rate of interest.[3]

This is in effect a translation of Marshall into Keynes' somewhat more precise jargon, with three new points emphasized: that it is *prospective* yields which matter (and these depend on the state of confidence as well as on objective calculations of yield): that these must

---

[1] *Industrial Fluctuations*, Macmillan, 1929, p. 86.
[2] *The General Theory of Employment, Interest and Money*, Macmillan, 1936, Book IV, Chapter 12, ss. II and III.
[3] Ibid., Chapter 11, s. I, pp. 135–7.

be *discounted*, i.e. the more distant yields written down in computing their present value: and that they should be related to replacement cost. Keynes appears to have slipped without noticing it into an assertion that the discounted expected yields *are in fact* set against the replacement cost (and not the market price of the asset), which is much more dubious. But it will be seen that he considers it 'obvious' that it is the rate of interest which fixes the boundary line to which the use of capital is pushed.

But elsewhere Keynes gives a much less precise description of business decisions, which fits ill with his main analysis:

> Most, probably, of our decisions to do something positive, the full consequences of which will be drawn out over many days to come, can only be taken as a result of animal spirits—of a spontaneous urge to action rather than inaction, and not as the outcome of a weighted average of quantitative benefits multiplied by quantitative probabilities. Enterprise only pretends to itself to be mainly actuated by the statements in its own prospectus, however candid and sincere. Only little more than an expedition to the South Pole, is it based on an exact calculation of benefits to come. . . .[1]

Furthermore, he knew very well that the calculation of yield is precarious and frequently impossible, and that many ventures are undertaken without a cold and rational calculation of profit:

> Our knowledge of the factors which will govern the yield of an investment some years hence is usually very slight and often negligible. If we speak frankly, we have to admit that our basis of knowledge for estimating the yield ten years hence of a railway, a copper mine, a textile factory, the goodwill of a patent medicine, an Atlantic liner, a building in the City of London amounts to little and sometimes to nothing; or even five years hence. In fact, those who seriously attempt to make any such estimate are often so much in the minority that their behaviour does not govern the market.[2]

Through this inconvenient complexity, however, he hacked his way by an analytical device: he defined an entrepreneur's expectation of proceeds as being that expectation 'which, if it were held with certainty, would lead to the same behaviour as does the bundle of vague and more various possibilities which actually makes up his state of expectation when he reaches his decision'.[3] So likewise Hicks[4] admits that people rarely have precise expectations, but he

---

[1] *The General Theory of Employment, Interest and Money*, Book IV, Chapter 12, s. VII, pp. 161–2.
[2] Ibid., Book, VI, Chapter 12, s. III, pp. 149–50.
[3] Ibid., Book I, Chapter 3, s. I, p. 24 (footnote).
[4] *Value and Capital*, pp. 125–6.

makes use of the analytical device of a 'most probable price' with an 'adjustment' for risk; thus he supposes that an analysis which deals in precise expectations is 'not altogether incompetent for dealing with a world in which risk is supremely important'.

The form of the Keynesian analysis led to a strong emphasis on the controlling power of the rate of interest, and thus of Government control over the amount of money. But in a celebrated paragraph Keynes expressed doubts (which have been magnified by his followers) about the adequacy of the rate of interest as a means of controlling investment:

> For my own part I am now somewhat sceptical of the success of a merely monetary policy directed towards influencing the rate of interest. I expect to see the State, which is in a position to calculate the marginal efficiency of capital-goods on long views and on the basis of the general social advantage, taking an ever greater responsibility for directly organising investment; since it seems likely that the fluctuations in the market estimation of the marginal efficiency of different types of capital, calculated on the principles I have described above, will be too great to be offset by any practicable changes in the rate of interest.[1]

This is not meant as a denial of the doctrines of his earlier chapters; it is an assertion that the psychological element in investment decisions may cause fluctuations too violent to be offset by variations in the rate of interest. This assertion of the primacy of an ill-defined state of sentiment brings him much nearer to reality. But Keynes does not seem to have inquired how physical investment decisions were in fact being made at the time when he wrote his book; he was more interested in the financial decisions of Stock Exchange operators. He appears also to have over-estimated the degree of independence of investment and saving; in the post-war period it has become more obvious that businesses, both small and large, often finance much of their investment from their own savings, and the decisions to invest and save cannot be regarded as independent. Some studies which we have seen of the finance of public companies (not yet published)[2] suggests, however, that the relation between the investment and saving habits of a particular company is surprisingly slight.

Three years after *The General Theory* there appeared another

[1] *The General Theory of Employment, Interest and Money*, Book IV, Chapter 12, s. VIII, p. 164.

[2] See p. 61 above, footnote 2.

major work, J. R. Hicks on *Value and Capital*. In a theoretical chapter on 'Interest and the Production Plan' he states '. . . the only important thing which emerges is the general conclusion . . . that changes in the rate of interest affect the tilt or *crescendo* of the production plan.'[1] But here the practical man emerges with some very important points:

So long as we are concerned with movements in rates of interest which fall within the ordinary range of such movements (say between 2 per cent and 7 per cent per annum), the effects of such changes on the discounted prices of outputs or inputs due for dates in the near future will be very slight. . . . But this same principle holds at the other extreme; when an output or input is planned for a date very far in the future, its discounted price becomes extremely sensitive to changes in the rate of interest. Consequently, the more of these distant outputs or inputs the plan contains, the more sensitive to interest it will be. . . .

The length of time for which an entrepreneur will be prepared to plan ahead depends partly upon technical conditions . . ., but it also depends, in a very important way, on risk. As we have often seen, the effective 'expected price' of a future output—the price at which it has to be estimated for purposes of the plan—is not the most probable price, but the most probable price *minus* an allowance for risk. Now the father ahead the future output is, the larger this risk-allowance is likely to become, just because the uncertainty of the future price increases; after a certain point, therefore, the risk-allowance will become so large as to wipe out any possible gains. . . . This is what brings the plan to an end, and prevents it extending into the indefinite future; but the plan is not merely cut short after a certain length of time; even those only relatively distant outputs whose 'expected prices' are not quite abolished by risk, are nevertheless gravely weakened in their influence on the plan by this writing-down due to risk. . . . But it is these very outputs upon whose *pull* interest must mainly rely, if it is to cause large adjustments in the plan; we now see that their *pull* is likely to be much less strong than we might have expected.

Interest is too weak for it to have much influence on the near future; risk is too strong to enable interest to have much influence on the far future; what place is left for interest between these opposing perils? How far it can find a place depends upon the strength of the risk factor; and that, as we have seen, is largely a psychological question. In a state of grave mistrust, people will 'live from hand to mouth'; if they do so, changes in the rate of interest (the moderate changes we are talking about) can have little influence on their conduct. In a state of confidence, on the other hand, risk-allowances are much smaller; and a space will probably be left between the

[1] *Value and Capital*, p. 224.

extremes where interest is ineffective, within which it can have a significant influence, of the kind we have analysed in this chapter.[1]

In general, however, Hicks' assumptions about uncertainty and expectations are, as he says, interpreted 'in a strict and rigid way, assuming that every individual has a definite idea of what he expects any price which concerns him to be in any future week'.[2] This he admits to be unrealistic, but his main interest is not in what business men do but in making headway in abstract dynamic theory.

Very shortly after the publication of *The General Theory*, the erosion of the Keynesian position began. Mr. P. W. S. Andrews and the Oxford Economists' Research Group were unable to find, by inquiries among business men, much evidence of any response to investment to changes in the rate of interest.[3] To explain this, Professor G. L. S. Shackle analysed the possibility that (except in certain special cases such as housing) uncertainty would normally swamp the effects of rate of interest changes.[4] The new evidence fell on receptive ears, and it was soon an article of faith among those followers of Keynes who believed in a Government-planned economy that monetary policy was of no use whatever in controlling investment, and consequently (since they accepted the necessity to regulate investment) that the control must be exercised by a planning authority.

The logic of this belief is weak; there may be instruments of control or direction which do not depend on the rate of interest, and which cannot be described as central planning; and the evidence of the lack of influence of rates of interest might prove misleading in altered circumstances. In a sense, the new attitude was a retreat to vagueness, an admission that we do not know how and why investment decisions are made. Even in the Keynesian system, the very relevant and important references to 'expectations' are an evasion of the issue, for if we do not know how expectations are formed and altered we are in effect without a theory of investment decisions. It is true that on the general theory of expectations the post-war years have seen the development of the highly original and important

[1] *Value and Capital*, pp. 225–6.
[2] Ibid., p. 124.
[3] P. W. S. Andrews, 'A Further Inquiry into the Effects of Rates of Interest', *Oxford Economic Papers*, March 1940, pp. 33–73.
[4] 'Interest-Rates and the Pace of Investment', *Economic Journal*, 1946, reprinted in *Uncertainty in Economics and other Reflections*, Cambridge University Press, 1955. See the quotation from Hicks, p. 116 above.

ideas of Professor Shackle,[1] but these have not yet received much practical application to business investment.

An independent attack on the traditional theories of investment decisions has been made in America by Professor A. G. Hart.[2] He has made it clear that to analyse business planning in terms of expectation schedules, constructed by discounting estimated receipts for each date under particular contingencies and weighting by the estimated probability of each contingency, forces us into unacceptable assumptions about the business man's attitude—that he concerns himself with no aspects of the probability distributions he is dealing with except their mean or expected values, and that he works out a business plan in full at the initial planning period and fixes it for the life of the firm, so ignoring the possibility of preserving flexibility.

The controversy about the effects of the rate of interest is a by-product of theories which were given an exact form as a convenience of analysis. The consequence of attempted precision is the making of indefensible assumptions. In the Keynesian theory, for instance, there are five assumptions:

1 that it is possible to make estimates in money terms of expected yields of an investment in all future periods of its life; or at least of the present value of the expected yields (i.e. after writing down or 'discounting' the future yields according to their remoteness);

2 that these estimates being possible, they are in fact made;

3 that they are compared, not with the market price of the investment-asset, but with its replacement cost;

4 that a decision to invest follows if the comparison shows that a money profit will be made;

5 that the rate of time-discount used in calculating the present value of the expected yields is identical with 'the' market rate of interest.

The first two of these are obviously essential in the statement of the theory which we have given above, and the third has already been mentioned. The fourth is another way of expressing the comparison of the marginal efficiency of capital with the rate of interest; for if the discounted expected future yields are greater than the cost of the

---

[1] *Expectation in Economics*, Cambridge University Press, 1949   *Uncertainty and Business Decisions*, 2nd edition, Liverpool University Press, 1957.

[2] *Anticipations, Uncertainty and Dynamic Planning*, New York, A. M. Kelley Inc., 1951.

asset, this is another way of saying that a higher rate of discount (i.e. a higher marginal efficiency) would be needed to bring the yields to equality with the cost of the asset. But the condition that investment is pushed just to the point where the marginal efficiency equals the market rate of interest requires the fifth assumption, that the market rate determines the rate of time-discount, or the 'average yield rate' corresponding to the expected future yields. This is an assumption of rationality by the investor; if the investment he will 'just' undertake yields 3 per cent, when 4 per cent can be obtained by an investment in the stock markets, he is acting irrationally in failing to seize the opportunity of greater profit.

These five assumptions are severally doubtful, and collectively wholly implausible, except in a minority of investment decisions of an exceptional kind. Rough money calculations of yield are some-times made, but not universally; in any case they are summaries of a whole complex of alternative possibilities, and to talk of *the* expected yield misses the interesting problem, which is how (if at all) the complex can be reduced to a single estimate of yield. The pursuit of profit, though an important feature of Western economic systems, cannot be assumed to govern every action in detail; and business men cannot be assumed to be making constant comparisons of widely different ways of employing their money, or even to be capable of 'switching' to a more profitable use. The market rate of interest forces itself upon the consciousness of a Keynes in his frequent opera-tions on the Stock Exchange; but to another business man it may come into the foreground only when there is a need to borrow from the market—and many firms go for years living on their own sav-ings, without any outside borrowing.

It would certainly be convenient if a money criterion could be found for every decision, and preferably one which expresses the attractiveness of any course of action by a simple figure, so that all the money-measures could be arranged in order in a line and a definite choice made of the most profitable. The possibility of 'summing up' a course of action by a single figure is, however, far from obvious. Professor Shackle in his treatment of decisions under uncertainty uses a two-dimensional criterion, and this has recently been considered as one among a more general set of possibilities.[1] The analysis which we have made in this book does not raise hopes of the possibility of making a simple and tidy theory, or even of the

[1] C. F. Carter in second edition of *Uncertainty and Business Decisions*, Liverpool University Press, 1957.

possibility of *approximating* to the truth by means of a simple model. The decision by many economists to obtain analytical simplicity by devices which get rid of uncertainty and other complications seems to us to have diverted the study of investment decisions into regions more productive of controversy than of enlightenment.

Index

New Manager's Library

Information on three other titles
in this series is given on the following pages.

The Practice of General Management
Catering Applications

DAVID A. FEARN

The author of this book has produced a simple and
eminently readable account of the management function in
the service industries.

In the course of his experience in the hotel trade he felt that
though many books were available on such topics as kitchen
planning, and management accounting no single book
considered these management techniques in relationship to
one another within the management system. Accordingly, he
has written this book in an attempt to explain how
management is effective by doing things through people,
what things are done, and how they are done successfully.
Each management function is broken down and examined,
then put back together and placed in perspective.

Because the book discusses basic management techniques it
has an applicability far greater than the limited field its title
suggests, and though models are drawn from the catering
trade this in no way detracts from the principles expounded.

356 03414 3

Profit Management and Control

FRED V. GARDENER

The innovation of the 'profitgraph' would by itself make this book worth studying. But it goes considerably further in break-even analysis as a control device, with reasonably complete instructions on how to use it.

One of the more useful insights, on which the profitgraph rests, is the analysis of capital into its float and variable factors.

356 03637 5

Direct Standard Costs
for Decision Making and Control

WILMER WRIGHT

This book is dedicated to the purpose of bridging the gap
between conservative accounting methods and the needs of
operating management. The author is convinced that the
potential value of direct standard cost accounting is so great
that every manager should insist that it be given a
hearing.

Direct standard cost accounting has one simple aim: to
ensure better profits. It does this through a programme of
dynamic profit planning and control. It provides strict
budgetary regulation, encourages forward planning, and
avoids post mortems and the development of alibi
artists.

The methods and procedures described in this book have
been tested in a great many companies and in a wide
variety of industries. Although the system is ideally suited to
the needs of small business, some of the largest corporations
in the world have applied it with equal success.

356 03638 3